WIMP JUNCTION

*The Place Your Sale
Was Lost ... and
How to Win It Back*

BY JENNICA DIXON
& TERRY SLATTERY

Published by Slattery Sales Group
808 Carmichael Rd #252, Hudson, WI 54016-7759
info@slatterysales.com | www.slatterysales.com

Slattery Sales Group books are available for bulk purchases for sales promotions, premiums, fundraising, and educational needs. For details and permission requests, write to the email address above.

This book does not claim to provide legal or financial advice. This book does not guarantee any results or earnings. Some names and identifying characteristics have been changed to protect the privacy of the individuals and companies involved.

ISBN 979-8-9891733-0-3 (Paperback)
ISBN 979-8-9891733-1-0 (eBook)
ISBN 979-8-9891733-2-7 (Audiobook)

Printed in the United States of America

Edited by Jessica Anderson
Cover Art by WaterKress Creative
Book Design by Toni Serofin, Sanserofin Studio

Book Website: www.wimpjunction.com

DOWNLOAD OUR FREE WIMP JUNCTION WORKBOOK AT
WWW.WIMPJUNCTION.COM/WORKBOOK
AND START BUILDING VALUABLE SALES ASSETS TO HELP
STREAMLINE AND ENHANCE YOUR SELLING EFFORTS
IN THE MARKETPLACE.

This book is dedicated to our clients in over 2,400 companies and 170 industries who have shared the impact of Wimp Junction on their business with us, giving us honest feedback as we refined these concepts and made them stronger. This work is for you. Thank you.

Contents

JUNCTION:
The place where two routes diverge:
your route to close your sale at high value,
and your prospect's route to commoditize you.

WIMP:
To unintentionally surrender value
and margins in a complex sale by taking
the prospect's route instead of yours.

Foreword

The book you're reading is the culmination of everything we've taught at the Slattery Sales Group since our founding almost forty years ago.

Conventional wisdom says we should hold back some material, giving you just enough to whet your appetite and induce you to hire us as consultants to get the rest of the way to your goals.

But I want to equip you with everything we possibly can so you can compete more effectively in the marketplace as you sell your goods, services, and ideas at high value. You're doing important work, and this book is intended to thoroughly — not partially — support your pursuit of fabulously lofty goals. I hope you find it so useful, both strategically and tactically, that you don't need us.

My father, Terry Slattery, founded the Slattery Sales Group when I was two years old, and both of my parents had had careers in high-tech sales before that. I grew up immersed in the sales and sales training industries. Like many children of entrepreneurs, I chose another career path entirely (banking and finance) to avoid sales and the family business.

But I became aware, over time, that the beautiful, organic, and necessary art of selling that I took for granted is dangerously underappreciated in the marketplace. My return to the sales industry was largely driven by my desire to support and equip the elite sellers, leaders, founders, and CEOs as they do the difficult work of convincing other humans to adopt something new.

So if you're convincing other humans to adopt something new (whether goods, services, or ideas), especially in the arena of complex sales, this book is for you. I hope we can help support and enhance your efforts.

At the Slattery Sales Group, we've helped over 2,400 companies compete more effectively through strategic differentiation so they can command high value against lower-priced competitors. And we've helped thousands of salespeople enhance their skills to run conversations so they can close more opportunities in less time and at higher margins.

I've personally watched the lives of countless individuals change dramatically because of the enhancements they learned from us at Slattery. I've seen founders finally exit the companies they built from scratch and executives salvage entire divisions from failure to thriving success. I've seen CEOs bring a brilliant new thing to the market and keep it there. And most satisfyingly, I've seen individual contributors lift their entire families to financial freedom. (Some of them even tell us we saved their marriages along the way as they adopted the Communication Keys we teach in Chapter 6; those are my favorite client testimonials!)

May this book be an evergreen source of insights, tactics, and wisdom for you as you do the beautiful, necessary, and difficult work of selling in the marketplace.

Jennica Dixon

Introduction to Wimp Junction

You've been pursuing this opportunity for months. You've meticulously researched the enterprise and their needs. You've prospected; you've networked; you've gotten past gatekeepers. You've landed various meetings with different role players and navigated your way through the organization until you finally got a meeting with the key decision-maker you've been targeting all along.

In that meeting with this key decision-maker, you expertly position your solution in the context of their needs; they agree it might solve some problems, and they'd like to know more. They ask if you can come back with more information so they might make an informed decision, and you reply, "Yes, absolutely."

You return to the office in triumph and move the opportunity forward in your Customer Relationship Management (CRM) system to reflect your progress toward presenting your solution. You spend all day Saturday writing the proposal and tailoring the slide deck to optimize its fit for your prospect.

You arrive well-equipped and find that your prospect had gotten so interested in your solution that they'd invited additional colleagues to the meeting. You present your solution flawlessly: enough information to impress, not enough to overwhelm or bore. They ask great questions, which you answer with ease. Your pricing is reasonably attractive: high enough to reflect your multifaceted value yet low enough to be competitive, considering everything your solution offers.

They tell you they liked it and that they will need some time to confer and think it over before coming to a decision; they will get back to you very soon. You leave the meeting elated at the prospect of an imminent closing, and you move the opportunity forward in your CRM system once more, this time to 80% likelihood. The next step will be to send the contract down to Legal for redlining, and then signing. So close!

Now you wait for them to respond, as they said they would.

And you wait.

And you wait.

When they still haven't reached out to you after a reasonable period of time, you give them a call. Your decision-maker doesn't answer, so you leave a voicemail. To be safe, you drop them an email too. It's the best email you've ever written.

And you wait.

And you wait.

But you never hear back.

Welcome to Wimp Junction.

The Story of Wimp Junction

My father, Terry Slattery, founded the Slattery Sales Group in 1985. Within two years, the business was on the brink of ruin along with similar enterprises in our franchise network around the country. The failure rate among our fellow franchisees was heading for a heartbreaking 90% and showed no sign of turning — until one day in 1987, when the concept of "Wimp Junction" came to my father like a sudden shower of rain in a parched desert. In a moment, he was inspired to describe at what point a complex sale is lost: in a figurative place he calls Wimp Junction.

No one had ever articulated the loss of a complex sale like this before, and it resonated immediately and deeply in the marketplace. It was so valuable to our clients (and all the referrals they sent us!) that it completely turned our business around.

My father shared the concept with some of his fellow franchisees who were also on the brink, and allowed them to teach and distribute the concept. They continue to tell him today that Wimp Junction saved their businesses.

Today, Wimp Junction is still the core of everything we do in our sales consulting firm. With it, we help elite salespeople stop getting stuck at Wimp Junction so their opportunities progress faster and they can close nine out of every ten opportunities they put on the table. With it, we help founders and CEOs establish simple, replicable, scalable sales processes so they can build a sales team that consistently wins in the marketplace at high margins. And with it, we help sales executives lead their enterprises with fiction-free forecasts and painless growth.

In this book, I will share the secrets of Wimp Junction along with the wisdom we've gained from supporting more than 2,400 companies over the last four decades. If you're a seller, my goal is to help you avoid Wimp Junction so you can close more opportunities, at higher margins, faster — and make a lot of money along the way. If you're a subject-matter expert or account manager, my goal is to help you run your conversations smoothly so you can sell the concepts for which you need consensus from your colleagues or clients. And if you're a sales executive, founder, or CEO, my goal is to equip you with the language and strategy you need to begin lifting performance in your sales organization so your growth is painless and your forecasts are fiction-free.

Let's dive in.

CHAPTER ONE

What's Really Happening at Wimp Junction

BUYING SYSTEMS

When a buyer and a seller meet in the marketplace, there are not one but two sales happening concurrently.

The salesperson is trying to convince the buyer that their differentiators have value. The buyer, meanwhile, is trying to convince the salesperson that what they're selling is a commodity and that their valuable differentiators are mere table stakes.

By the end of each meeting, one party will have advanced their sale one step further.

Companies spend significant money training their buyers (those in Procurement, Purchasing, Vendor Management, etc.) to extract discounts and concessions from salespeople. The buyers you encounter are trained, and they are good.

My father once saw an advertisement for a training seminar titled, "How to Protect Your Company from Highly Skilled Salespeople." Since he was a sales trainer, he thought it would be interesting to attend, and indeed it was. The full-day session taught tips and strategies to buyers from various companies to defend against (and milk concessions from) the salespeople who knock on their doors.

When the session was done, my father introduced himself to the trainer and discovered that this man had started out as a sales trainer too — but had changed direction upon learning that companies were willing to pay much, much more to train their buyers than they would ever pay to train their sellers. Thus, he now trained buyers.

Those buyers, a.k.a. your prospects, are trained to protect themselves from salespeople. This is particularly true in complex sales, in which larger enterprises are more likely to have players in focused buying roles. Every time you meet with a prospect in a complex sale, remember that they are probably trained; they follow a buying system, and it's engineered to annihilate your margins.

The prospect's buying system is what you encounter at Wimp Junction: the place the sale is lost.

The Prospect's System

STEP 1

The prospect lies to the salesperson.

STEP 2

The prospect gets the salesperson to provide valuable information and a quote.

STEP 3

The prospect lies about what's going to happen next.

STEP 4

The prospect doesn't answer or return the salesperson's calls.

WIMP JUNCTION: *What's Really Happening*

When my father was a small boy during World War II, he often accompanied his grandfather to work. Grandpa Kopp was a railroad engineer who packed a limburger-and-onion sandwich for lunch each morning and conducted trains until evening. My young father was enthralled by the powerful engines and smooth railroad tracks, so it's not surprising that his metaphor here, Wimp Junction, takes its inspiration from trains.

Let's imagine that your sale is like a train, chugging forward along its tracks until suddenly, the tracks split into two, and you find yourself traveling on the wrong set of tracks, heading away from your original destination. You're not entirely sure how you got there — in fact, the junction was so smooth that you don't even remember being diverted — but you're miles away from where you'd hoped to be in your journey. Maybe you find yourself in a last-minute price war at the end of a sale that was so close to signing. Maybe your prospect is in their fifth month of "thinking it over." Maybe you're being forced to answer to the new committee who's taking weeks to pull apart your value proposition, not realizing how much it's costing them to undervalue what you bring.

Wimp Junction is where a sale is diverted from one destination (yours) to another destination (the buyer's). It's the place the sale is lost — and it often happens much earlier on the route than people think.

Let's revisit our earlier scenario to break down what's really happening at Wimp Junction.

STEP #1

You've been pursuing this opportunity for months. You've meticulously researched the enterprise and their needs. You've prospected; you've networked; you've gotten past gatekeepers. You've landed various meetings with different role players and navigated your way through the organization until you finally got a meeting with the key decision-maker you've been targeting all along.

In that meeting with this key decision-maker, you expertly position your solution in the context of their needs; they agree it might solve some problems, and they'd like to know more.

STEP #1
IN THE PROSPECT'S BUYING SYSTEM
The prospect lies to the salesperson.

Your prospects are lying to you. (If you're from the nice Midwestern United States, please reread that sentence out loud twenty times.)

Prospects aren't necessarily lying to you all the time — only when their lips are moving. When their lips are moving, you can assume they are lying to you.

Can we blame them? We all lie to salespeople because we don't like being sold to. (It's a common maxim in the marketplace that people "hate to be sold to, but love to buy.") So, we lie to get out of engaging with salespeople. When you're in the marketplace, you might hear a dismissive lie that sounds like, "No, we don't need what you're selling." In fact, they probably do need what you're selling; but they don't want to be sold to, and something tripped their anti-salesperson defenses (probably a premature pitch from you or a colleague), and they've disengaged.

Another reason prospects lie is to inflate their authority, and it sounds like this: "I'm the decision-maker." But when you're in a complex sale, they aren't — there's never one decision-maker in a complex sale. Those prospects will lie to you about their authority to keep you from finding out how their decision will really be made (generally outside of their domain).

But the most common and dangerous reason prospects lie is this: They lie to you in order to engage you and commoditize you. It sounds like this: "Yes, I'm interested." They're not actually interested; you haven't uncovered any real motivation to change yet, let alone any real motivation to buy something from you. But they tell you they're interested so you'll move on to Step #2 with them.

STEP #2

They ask if you can come back with more information so they might make an informed decision, and you reply, "Yes, absolutely." You return to the office in triumph and move the opportunity forward in your CRM to reflect your progress toward presenting your solution. You spend all day Saturday writing the proposal and tailoring the slide deck to optimize its fit for your prospect.

You arrive well-equipped and find that your prospect had gotten so interested in your solution that they'd invited additional colleagues to the meeting. You present your solution flawlessly: enough information to impress, not enough to overwhelm or bore. They ask great questions, which you answer with ease. Your pricing is reasonably attractive: high enough to reflect your multifaceted value yet low enough to be competitive, considering everything your solution offers.

STEP #2

IN THE PROSPECT'S BUYING SYSTEM

The prospect gets the salesperson to provide valuable information and a quote.

In Step #2, your prospect gets you to provide valuable information and pricing, usually in the form of a presentation, demo, proposal, or quote.

At Slattery, we call this step Unpaid Consulting. And as my father, Terry, says, unpaid consultants live short, stressful lives and raise skinny children. If you're doing consulting in the marketplace, we want you to get paid for it.

Note: This step (providing valuable information and a quote) is not limited to just "The Big Presentation of an Offer to Do Business" at the end of your sale — sellers slide into Step #2 here all the time with miniature pitches along the way, usually unprompted. They talk about their solution and its features, benefits, and pricing. Those premature pitches land them solidly in Step #2 whether they intended to do a presentation or not.

There is a right time to offer all the details of your solution to a qualified prospect; we'll talk more about the qualification process later, in Chapter 7. But ultimately, going to Step #2 with an "interested" prospect is walking into Unpaid Consulting. In this step, they're extracting valuable information from you. Where might they go with it?

STEP #3

They tell you they liked it and that they will need some time to confer and think it over before coming to a decision; they will get back to you very soon.

STEP #3
IN THE PROSPECT'S BUYING SYSTEM
The prospect lies about what's going to happen next.

Remember Step #1, when we concluded that prospects lie? They're probably lying here too — this time about what's going to happen next.

It will sound like this: "Gee, this looks really interesting. We're going to have to ... think it over."

At Slattery, we're out to kill Think It Overs, or TIOs. TIOs are deadly; they lengthen the sales cycle, costing you valuable margin dollars, and ultimately, your opportunity. Our own experience in the marketplace indicates that about 40% of all offers from sellers result in no decision at all — not even to a competitor. This means sellers are spending enormous amounts of time and resources educating prospects who aren't thinking it over because they have no intention of making a change at all.

Yet they got you to provide valuable information and a quote ... so what might your prospect actually be doing in this time when they say they're thinking it over?

They're probably taking the information you so generously provided in Step #2 (Unpaid Consulting) and bringing it to your competitors. They're comparing solutions and asking for discounts. They're especially doing this with their incumbent because they can now drive a harder bargain with that provider using the information they extracted from you.

They may also be using the information you provided to design or enhance their own in-house solution so they can avoid going through the pain of change altogether.

But they're definitely not "thinking it over."

STEP #4

You leave the meeting elated at the prospect of an imminent closing, and you move the opportunity forward in your CRM system once more, this time to 80% likelihood. The next step will be to send the contract down to Legal for redlining, and then signing. So close!

Now you wait for them to respond, as they said they would.

And you wait.
And you wait.

When they still haven't reached out to you after a reasonable period of time, you give them a call. Your decision-maker doesn't answer, so you leave a voicemail. To be safe, you drop them an email, too. It's the best email you've ever written.

And you wait.

And you wait.

But you never hear back.

STEP #4
IN THE PROSPECT'S BUYING SYSTEM
The prospect doesn't answer or return
the salesperson's calls.

At this point, there's only one person who doesn't realize that this opportunity has concluded: you, the salesperson. The prospect has no intention of calling you back; they are not thinking it over.

Many salespeople react to Step #4 with increasingly fervent efforts to close the deal. Many sales leaders, facing a pipeline full of deals stuck at Step #4, start looking to hire a "closer" to get these deals moving again.

Here's the danger of being stuck at Step #4: Desperate salespeople and leaders are vulnerable to offering discounts or concessions in a last-ditch effort to wrap up a stuck opportunity. Prospects don't care about quarter-end forecasts and will remain dark for as long as it's advantageous for them. (The longer they wait, the greater the discount they might be offered!)

As we mentioned in Step #3, they're probably bringing the information to your competitors to extract better concessions from everybody, especially from the incumbent.

But there's another, equally dangerous, possibility: They're ready to make a change, and they're taking the information you provided and putting it onto a spreadsheet. Your valuable information has now become column fodder. Every solution looks like an interchangeable commodity on those spreadsheets, and your margins have gone virtual. Pretty soon the prospect concludes they have enough information to issue a Request for Proposals (RFP) later next year, and you'll get an invitation to join.

Remember this about RFPs: Your prospect is holding a luau, and they're looking for a pig.

Your prospects have a buying system, and it's engineered to commoditize you. When you hit Wimp Junction, you must take another track or risk becoming column fodder for RFPs and bidding wars. Your margins are too important to risk losing to the prospect's buying system.

YOUR MARGINS AND THE DOOM OF DISCOUNTING

Margins (or profits) are the mother's milk of any enterprise; margins are what allow the enterprise to grow and ultimately survive. Healthy and consistent margins are critical to the longevity of your business.

The colossal danger of discounting is this: The first, and often only, casualty of discounting is margins. We can't reduce the cost to produce our solution, but we can reduce the profits earned on it when we sell at a lower price.

When we discount our solution and sell at lower margins, we must make up the difference with higher volume if our enterprise is to survive at all.

However, it takes a surprising increase in volume to make up the margin dollars that were discounted away. It's not a simple linear relationship in which a 10% discount requires a 10% increase in volume to make up margin dollars; rather, we must sell a disproportionately higher volume in order to make up the difference in lost margins.

Offering a 10% discount on something that normally sees a 25% profit margin doesn't mean we have to sell 10% more to make up the difference — it means *we must sell 67% more* to bring the same number of margin dollars back to our company.

Allow me to use an example to illustrate:

Let's say we manufacture widgets and sell them for $5,000 each. Our profit margin is 25%, which means we earn $1,250 margin dollars on every widget we sell. Thus, it costs us $3,750 to produce every widget we make. This cost won't change.

Our star salesperson lands a new account and sells a widget for $5,000. At a 25% profit margin, we earn $1,250 in margin dollars, and we spend $3,750 to produce it. Business is good.

But our star salesperson starts getting stuck at Wimp Junction, and prospects begin pressuring them for discounts. A major prospect tells that salesperson, "I can get widgets exactly like yours from any of your competitors, and they'll sell them to me at a lower price. Can you give me a 10% discount?"

The salesperson has a high need to be liked and doesn't want to offend this prospect, so they say, "Sure, let me see what I can do." They request a 10% discount from the home office, and unfortunately their sales manager (enthralled at the idea of new revenue to fill a deficient pipeline) approves it.

So the next widget is sold at a 10% discount, for $4,500 (rather than the $5,000 it should have been).

But here's the catch: *It still costs us $3,750 to produce that widget!* This means that the 10% discount comes *entirely* out of margin dollars. Instead of the $1,250 we would have earned without discounting, we now earn just $750 in margin dollars. That's a steep 40% drop in profit!

In order to get back up to quota (the original $1,250 of margin dollars they're expected to bring in), the salesperson must make up the difference with higher volume — more sales transactions. But bringing in those margin dollars is now much harder at the new lower price because the profit margin has dropped to 17% on each discounted sale. (And yes, there will be more discounted sales because prospects talk to each other, and word gets out that discounts are available. Suddenly, all new prospects, and even some existing clients, are pushing for a 10% discount!)

So our star salesperson must head out to the marketplace again and sell more widgets to recover the margin dollars they discounted away. At the new lower 17% profit margin, recovering $500 of margins now requires a whopping $3,000 in new sales ($3,000 new sales x 17% profit margin = $500 margin).

That's an additional 67% in volume *above* the $4,500 they just sold! ($3,000 = 67% x $4,500)

Let's translate that 67% increase to your sales: If your quota for the year is to make ten sales (at full price), you now need to *close seventeen sales* in order recoup the margin dollars lost by discounting. If your quota is one hundred sales, you'll need to *close 167 sales* to bring in the exact same margin dollars you would have earned without discounting. Do you see the inherent doom in discounting?

Even a small discount represents a significant shift in strategy to higher-volume sales. Unfortunately for our star salesperson, higher-volume sales are more efficiently won with effective marketing efforts — not with slow, expensive human salespeople.

Discounting is deadly to your quota, your margins, and your enterprise — and ultimately to your own role.

The buyers you meet with are trained to commoditize you — and that's exactly what they will try to do. If you start following their buying system, you will find yourself at Wimp Junction facing pressures to offer discounts and concessions. Our goal here is to help you protect your margins, avoid Wimp Junction, and confidently sell your solution at high value.

CHAPTER TWO

What is Selling?

THE ART OF SELLING

Since the concept of selling is foundational to everything we're going to do together in this book, let's begin by defining the word.

Selling is an art that is often misunderstood. Most of what is referred to as "selling" (usually with some downward jeer) isn't actually selling.

Selling is, quite simply, the art of consensual cooperation — the art of persuading another human being to change what they're doing, with both their cooperation and their consent.

Human cooperation is the foundation of market exchange. Humans cooperate with each other, as they have since the dawn of recorded time, by exchanging in trade, whether trading beads for bread or cryptocurrency for digital art. Voluntary exchange doesn't happen without the cooperation and consent of both parties: Each one must value what they're *getting* more than what they're *giving up* (or they wouldn't be voluntarily trading it away).

If they won't be better off, then they probably won't consent to the exchange.

Humans can cooperate without consent, for example, when they accommodate the hostage-taker in a bank robbery, or pay taxes to their government whether they like it or not. But in the marketplace, consent is necessary to cooperation.

Prospects don't have to cooperate with us. They don't have to buy what we're selling. And we can't use force, fiat, or fraud to squeeze money from an unwilling prospect. If a prospect doesn't want to buy what we're selling, we can't lock them up (we're not the law); we can't confiscate their stuff (we're not the IRS); and we can't go break their kneecaps (we're not the Mafia). We must offer something of value in exchange.

In order to get their money — or even get them moving toward a conversation to discuss any kind of exchange at all — we need both their cooperation AND their consent.

If you don't have your prospect's cooperation, you have no sale. You're bound by their consent every step of the way. Thank goodness — that's what makes the marketplace a beautiful place of organic engagement. But it also makes our job difficult because we cannot push a prospect forward who doesn't want to budge.

The shady shenanigans we all associate with "selling" (trap closes, trial closes, hidden fees, inflated promises, and outright fraud) aren't true selling — they're cheap tricks to get around consent and cooperation in order to make up for poor goods or low skills.

This may sound simplistic, but it's absolutely foundational to everything we will do together in this book. Prospects are entrenched in their current habits and behaviors, and you're out to persuade them to try something new — and to part with their money while they're doing it. It's a difficult task, one made even harder when you can't move forward without their consent. Our sale ultimately has nothing to do with our awesome solution's features or benefits — instead, it has everything to do with the prospect's perception of the value we bring them.

The entire Slattery system of selling is oriented toward the prospect — their universe, their problems, their perspective — not because we're feeling empathetic for empathy's sake, but because our revenues and margins depend entirely on our ability to skillfully navigate the decisions made by the other autonomous humans throughout the exchange.

Oddly enough, this prospect-oriented selling system is what will help us avoid following the prospect's buying system at Wimp Junction. It will increase our awareness so we know exactly where we are relative to the prospect, all the time. It will help us discern those "interested" prospects who have no real motivation to change so we can conserve our selling resources and move on to more qualified opportunities faster. And it will help us translate our unique solution to their unique problems, allowing us to stand out and avoid commoditization.

Selling isn't about us and our solution — it's about the prospect and their perspective. What the prospect values is of immeasurable importance to the cadence of our sale. We must maintain unwavering focus on the prospect's perspective in order to move our sale toward closure at high value in less time.

THE LAST MILE

Much of what is called "selling" in the marketplace today isn't really selling — it's marketing, carried out inefficiently by a human with a slide deck. (Incidentally, those in-person marketing efforts tend to land sellers squarely onto the buyer's side of the tracks at Wimp Junction.)

Marketing is the art of getting your company's message about what you're selling into the marketplace. It's a strategic effort that might include branding, messaging, and advertising with print ads, online ads, billboards, product placements, radio commercials, blog posts, building signs, and more. Marketing tells the marketplace what you offer and how great it is.

Marketing is "one-to-many" — that is, one single message goes to many people. The same message is delivered to multiple potential prospects.

Selling, however, is a "one-to-one" effort — that is, one seller skillfully engages a human prospect through conversations that uncover the prospect's true motivation to change and that translate the marketing message to the prospect's world.

At Slattery, we call selling the "Last Mile" of making a sale, to persuade a prospect to change what they're doing. Marketing can get the message most of the way there into the prospect's world, but the Last Mile can only be traveled by foot as the human seller engages the human prospect in conversations.

Those conversations help the prospect become aware that things could be different or better; they uncover the prospect's actionable pain and real motivation to change; they reveal the complexities of the prospect's decision-making processes that can mire your sale;

and they drive your unique value to "must-have" status so you can win over someone else's lower price.

Marketing tells, but the seller sells. Marketing positions the concept; the seller leverages it. Marketing enables the conversation; the seller runs the conversation. Marketing tactics can be automated, but selling must always be done by a human.

Only a human salesperson can navigate the complicated terrain of prospect organizations, where competing interests, internal politics, and sheer busyness can bog down the decision-making process indefinitely.

At Slattery, we've seen a lot of trends come and go over the decades. Every few years, someone claims that the "death of the salesman" is imminent because of some hot new technology. In fact, technology may improve the ways we market and advertise and carry our message to the marketplace, but human salespeople will always be necessary to carry it the Last Mile, where conversations happen.

The length of the Last Mile will vary depending on the type of sale being conducted. Some simple transactional sales can be completed almost entirely with just marketing, as effective online funnels move consumers from "unaware" to "raving customer" with little human interaction, if any. In those sales, the Last Mile (if it exists at all) is relatively short — maybe one quick conversation between humans at the very end to close:

MARKETING
Introduces brand, product, or service.
Increases awareness. Persuades. Answers questions.

SELLING
"Last Mile"
conversations

But as the sale becomes more complex (perhaps the solution is more technical, or there are more key players in the cast of characters to engage, with complicated decision-making processes at the prospect organization and multiple conversations), then the Last Mile becomes increasingly crucial to closing the sale. Marketing can generate leads, help open initial conversations, and provide high-level explanations of the product or service, but the Last Mile requires considerable engagement and attention:

The balance between marketing and selling may shift one way or another over the life of a product or service. Many goods that were once sold almost entirely through human-to-human sales are now sold online with great marketing: vacuums, insurance, software, even cars. On the other hand, some enterprises find they now need to go beyond marketing and are bolstering their human sales teams for the Last Mile to compete effectively at high value.

Too often, we see enterprises make the deadly mistakes of undervaluing the skill and effort needed in the Last Mile and of assuming the marketplace will be as impressed with their solution's amazing features and benefits as they are. They send their sellers out with marketing material to wow prospects and tell them all about it (Step #2 at Wimp Junction — Unpaid Consulting!). They assume prospects will rationally conclude that it's in their enterprise's best interest to buy, and sales will come in.

But this approach unnecessarily slows down the selling cadence and extends cycle times because competitors are doing the exact same thing. They're sending sellers out with similar marketing materials, talking about similar features and benefits; prospects can't distinguish between the marketing messages. The prospect is left to collect, sort, and compare information from all the sellers before putting everything onto a spreadsheet, on which all solutions look alike, and eventually picking one, probably based on lowest price (if they decide at all).

Sometimes the prospect might choose to simplify everything by issuing an RFP, which will add another six to nine months to the entire selling process. It also drops the possibility of winning to about 3% at unsustainably low margins. (Again, the RFP is just a luau, and they're looking for a pig.)

To truly differentiate in the marketplace and sell at high value, we must navigate the Last Mile, carefully translating the marketing promises of our solution to the unique challenges our prospect is facing. We cannot trust the prospect do that translation because they don't have the time, bandwidth, or experience to do it.

We must also navigate the prospect's decision-making process and influence it so our unique edge is valued more than lowest price. We must maintain what military leaders call "situational awareness" at every step, so we know where we are and can avoid being pulled down to the prospect's side of the tracks at Wimp Junction. And we must stay in rapport with the prospect's commitment to solving their problems because if we become more committed than they are to their success, then we're vulnerable to the pressures of commoditization and discounts.

These Last Mile skills can never be replaced by an algorithm. Machines cannot make them obsolete. A human seller will always be necessary in complex sales because sellers go where marketing can't.

The point of selling isn't to get leads, educate prospects, or put marketing collateral in front them. The point of selling is to have the conversations in that Last Mile where marketing cannot go.

SELLING IN COMPLEX SALES

We use the term "complex sale" to refer to any sale in the marketplace that involves multiple buying parties and multiple discussions. This is different from a transactional sale, which can be accomplished in a single transaction with a single decision-maker. Complex sales are typically conducted business-to-business (B2B), that is, one enterprise selling to another enterprise.

When it comes to selling in complex B2B sales, many people assume that rational logic will win the day. Yes, we humans are finicky and irrational consumers, but enterprises make rational economic decisions, right? And when it's obviously in the enterprise's best interest to purchase the solution, then it'll be a straightforward win, right?

Unfortunately, enterprises are complex organisms. There are always more demands for funding than there are funds, and the decision of *what* gets funded *when* is ultimately made by finicky humans with wildly variable priorities and interests. This is what makes complex B2B sales fascinating, risky, rewarding, and, well ... complex!

Complex sales take longer to complete than a simple transactional sale. It can take anywhere from six to eighteen months between first contact and signed contract. In that time, various people at the prospect organization are managing their own internal risks of mistakes related to choosing the wrong solution. They're making complicated decisions regarding which initiatives to fund and why. They're also resolving conflicts between those who think everything is a commodity (and who think lowest price should always win), and those who know better and who want the solution with the lowest total cost over time.

It's very easy to mistake the silence of Wimp Junction for the natural delays of a complex sale, and some discernment is required here. We must maintain situational awareness, cultivate relationships with multiple players in the cast of characters in the right positions, maintain their goodwill, run conversations to drive our value into their decision-making processes, and always keep the cost of delay at the forefront of the conversation with each person involved so our sale continues its forward cadence.

Complex sales are also considerably more expensive to conduct; they require a significant investment of time, resources, and knowledge from you (the seller) and your company. Proposals may number in the hundreds of pages; presentations, site visits, and demos may happen over the course of many days or weeks. Because of this, it is crucial to regularly and astutely assess sales opportunities to determine whether or not they're worth pursuing.

With the stakes so high, it's critically important to avoid Wimp Junction in complex sales. The gravitational pull to discounting and commoditization is incredibly strong here, where enterprise buyers are very well-trained to run their buying systems and pull salespeople onto their side of the tracks at Wimp Junction.

As we mentioned above, 40% of all complex sales are done incorrectly and result in no decision (i.e., no sale at all, not even to a competitor). This means an enormous amount of selling resources are spent on deals that never even have a chance of closing — they're stuck indefinitely at Step #4 of Wimp Junction.

These wasted efforts, drained resources, and margin strains are avoidable. Complex sales require efficient execution, ruthless qualification, and internal discipline on the part of the seller and their enterprise so that selling resources are directed toward opportunities worth pursuing at a sustainable cadence.

WHY HAVE SALESPEOPLE IN A COMPLEX SALE?

We often ask CEOs when we begin working together, "Why does your company have salespeople?"

Common answers range from the obvious ("to close deals") to the mundane ("to open relationships," "to educate the prospects," "to gain top-of-mind awareness").

But those things can be accomplished more cost-effectively with marketing, advertising, and the nearly infinite ways to reach people electronically. We don't need salespeople for them.

Salespeople are expensive, and they're often difficult to manage. So why bother having them?

As we mentioned above, there's a difference between marketing and selling; that difference becomes even more pronounced in complex sales. With the increased costs, complications, and time horizons of complex sales, it becomes essential to have absolute clarity around exactly what a salesperson should be doing in that Last Mile of activity.

There are just two reasons for an enterprise to incur the headache and expense of having salespeople run the Last Mile in a complex sale:

1. To *learn* how your prospect makes their decision to do or not do business with you.

2. To *alter* that decision-making process until it places more value on your differentiators than on someone else's lower price.

First, let's discuss #1: *learning* how your prospect makes their decision to do or not do business with you.

In a simple transactional sale, you might ask, "Who's the decision-maker?"

But in a complex sale (as Terry learned selling enterprise solutions at IBM), that question is deadly — it will lead you down a rabbit hole of competing personalities at your prospect organization as you navigate the various characters all trying to protect their own agendas and assert that they are, in fact, your hallowed "decision-maker." (Remember, they're lying.)

In a complex sale, a decision is never made by a single person. A decision is always reached after much deliberation, consideration, conversation, and in some cases, complicated politicking. It is never as simple as "Who makes this decision?"

That's why we don't ask who the decision-maker is. Rather, "How will this decision be made?" is our key question. It takes into account all the various moving parts of a complex sale that can derail our efforts: the competing priorities, the pressing needs, the unspoken alliances, the old grudges between departments, that one board member whose cousin is CEO of our arch-competitor ... we can't afford to seek a single decision-maker.

We've done thousands of sales autopsies over the decades, and one thing stands firm: When a sale that was forecast at high confidence was lost in the late stages of the sale, nine times out of ten the loss happened because the seller did not fully understand HOW the decision would be made at the prospect organization. It's an absolute minefield in complex sales; there are too many variables that can take us out if we rely on one single decision-making channel.

We counsel our clients to stop using the term "decision-maker" entirely; that's how important it is to know HOW the decision will be made in a complex sale.

Think of it this way: If you ask, "Who?" you'll never get the "How." But if you ask, "How?" you'll always get the "Who" too.

Now let's discuss #2: The second reason to have salespeople is to *alter* that decision-making process so it places more value on our differentiators over someone else's lower price.

Our unique differentiators must become must-haves in our prospects' evaluation and decision-making processes. We cannot be pulled haplessly into their decision-making process, or we risk being commoditized by their criteria demanding lowest price (or anything other than our unique strengths).

If you achieve the first goal and learn how your prospect makes decisions, but you do not follow through and alter that decision-making process to favor your value, then you will find yourself unable to justify your higher pricing, and you will slide down to commodity status; you may even find yourself responding to RFPs that a competitor created.

This is the essence of how you avoid Wimp Junction and sell at high value in a complex sale: You must *learn* how your prospect will make their decision, and then you must *alter* that process so your value becomes a must-have over a competitor's lower price.

CHAPTER THREE

How to Avoid Wimp Junction

The Prospect's Buying System

Your System

STEP 1

The prospect lies to the salesperson.

STEP 2

The prospect gets the salesperson to provide valuable information and a quote.

STEP 3

The prospect lies about what's going to happen next.

STEP 4

The prospect doesn't answer or return the salesperson's calls.

WIMP JUNCTION®

STAGE 1
Differentiate

STAGE 2
Target

STAGE 3
Engage

STAGE 4
Commit

STAGE 5
Secure

In the next chapters, we will offer a map to the right side of the train tracks, where you can follow your own selling system instead of the prospect's buying system, thus avoiding Wimp

Junction. This will help you shrink your sales cycle, protect your margins, avoid Unpaid Consulting, qualify your prospects, and kill Think It Overs forever.

On the right side of the tracks, the Selling System we teach involves five stages: Differentiate, Target, Engage, Commit, and Secure. We'll discuss each of these in the following chapters, from both a strategic perspective (i.e., why each stage is important and what we're accomplishing there) and a tactical level (with methods and steps to help you execute it effectively). Whether you're in an established industry with entrenched competitors or in a brand-new market space where your only competitor is the status quo, these five stages will help bring situational awareness, clarity, and smooth flow to your side of the tracks so you can avoid Wimp Junction.

The system we teach is both "micro" and "macro." We say it's micro in the sense that it informs the substance and flow of your discrete sales calls with individual prospects, but it's also macro in the sense that it provides a strategic map to your opportunity as a whole and its likelihood of closure.

This system works. We've lifted performance in more than two thousand organizations using this system. Our clients tend to see a lift in margins first, because existing opportunities can be closed faster with our approach to strategic differentiation (our Stage 1 on the right side of the tracks). The typical margin lift is 8% above current margins (e.g., lift from 25% to 27% profit margin).

The next thing our clients see improve is top-line revenue, which typically rises about 25% as the pipeline fills with higher-quality opportunities. It's also not uncommon for our clients to set the internal expectation that their salespeople can and should be consistently closing nine out of ten offers they put on the table. When win rates are that high, it means our clients are limiting their engagement early when they realize they can't win and are instead focusing their limited time and resources pursuing winnable opportunities. (Conversely, when win rates are low, it means that sellers are pursuing for too long those opportunities that were probably never winnable; the wasted time and resources on those opportunities depresses margins unnecessarily.)

Implementing our system is not meant to be a painful rip-and-replace overhaul of your existing sales habits or processes — it is meant to enhance the good things you're already doing in your sales. If something is already working for you, continue doing it, and use our suggestions simply to augment those efforts.

Sometimes, when new clients are introduced to our system, they find themselves asking, "This is fantastic, but when do we actually sell?" This is because our system is prospect-oriented, with every step focused on the prospect and helping them move through the pain of change. What our new clients are really asking is, "When can we talk about us?"

And the answer is: Hopefully, you won't have to.

Let's begin.

CHAPTER FOUR

Differentiate

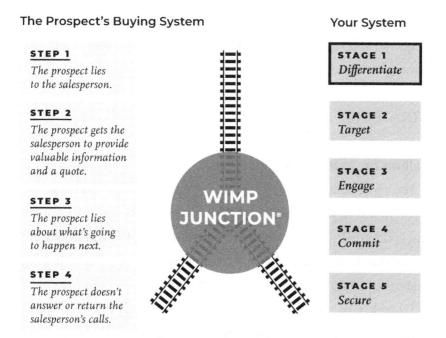

The Prospect's Buying System

STEP 1
The prospect lies to the salesperson.

STEP 2
The prospect gets the salesperson to provide valuable information and a quote.

STEP 3
The prospect lies about what's going to happen next.

STEP 4
The prospect doesn't answer or return the salesperson's calls.

Your System

STAGE 1
Differentiate

STAGE 2
Target

STAGE 3
Engage

STAGE 4
Commit

STAGE 5
Secure

Let's begin our Selling System at Stage 1: Differentiate. Differentiation is the most important concept to avoid being commoditized at Wimp Junction. We begin all our work with clients by helping them articulate what differentiates them in the marketplace so they can command premium value and mitigate the risks of being commoditized. This is the foundation of everything else we do together to stay on the right side of the railroad tracks.

In this chapter, we'll discuss the concept of strategic competitive differentiation. Then we'll walk through a tactical exercise to help you differentiate yourself from your competition and avoid Wimp Junction.

No matter how much work our clients have previously done on their differentiation, they always find this to be the most valuable work we do together; they come away with a stronger competitive edge and more powerful language, which they and their team can leverage in the Last Mile of selling.

STRATEGIC

Selling on Value Over Price

Your prospects will work hard to convince you that your solution looks just like your competitors'. They do this because they want the good stuff at the price of the not-so-good stuff, and they want to remove all risk of taking the cheap option. Their entire buying system is designed to commoditize you.

However, in any marketplace, there can be only one competitor with the lowest price. That competitor will typically be the lowest-cost producer, since they have pricing power.

Salespeople are expensive; if your enterprise has salespeople, you are probably not the lowest-cost producer. Thus, you cannot offer the lowest-priced solution and cannot compete on price.

Your only other option is to compete on value.

Value, in the way we define it, is the "something else" you bring to the marketplace to justify the higher-than-lowest price. At Slattery, we call it Differentiating Value, or DV.

Here are two truths about DV:

- Truth #1: Every competitor MUST bring something unique to the marketplace, or they risk becoming column fodder for bidding wars and RFPs (which don't require expensive salespeople). That "something unique" is their Differentiating Value.
- Truth #2: Those who have Differentiating Value and can articulate it so that prospects understand it and value it will win, even if their price is higher.

Those who don't have DV, don't know what theirs is, or can't articulate it (so prospects understand and value it) will be forced to compete on price. Such commoditization is deadly to your margins and ultimately to your enterprise.

With DV, you can win even when you're more expensive than your competitors because your DV brings value to your prospect, which will justify your higher price.

You may not think of your solution as being "high price" — in fact, you may think it's an absolute bargain for all its amazing features and the benefits it brings your clients. But from the prospect's perspective, they may think they can get the same fix cheaper or more easily elsewhere — and that's the perspective that matters in this exchange.

To command higher value and avoid being commoditized, we must sell on our Differentiating Value — not on our features and benefits. This will help us avoid the buyer's buying system at Wimp Junction.

The Foundation of DV: No Free Moves

When it comes to determining your Differentiating Value, No-Fail Selling Rule #1 governs everything: There are no free moves. Ever.

Every decision we make in life involves trade-offs, and trade-offs have consequences.

There is an opportunity cost embedded in every unique decision we make — we give up the next best option because we can't have both options at once.

There's an opportunity cost to your current choice of career, which you gave up to be where you are today; maybe you would have otherwise become an astronaut. If so, then not being an astronaut is your opportunity cost of being an elite seller.

NO-FAIL RULE #1
There are no free moves. Ever.
Every decision a prospect makes involves trade-offs.
Those trade-offs have consequences.
If you have DV, your prospect faces consequences
for not choosing you.

Every unique decision we make has an opportunity cost buried in it somewhere, either financial or otherwise. Thus, there are no free moves. Ever. This rule is key to understanding your Differentiating Value.

If you have DV, then someone, somewhere, is paying for not having it — in time, money, resources, mental load, opportunity cost, etc. — even though they don't know about you. If you have DV, then there are consequences to your prospect for not doing business with you — even if they've never heard of you.

In a world of no free moves, either your prospects are living with the consequences of not having your DV (which only you can provide in the marketplace), or you're hallucinating about your DV.

If you have DV, then your prospect faces real consequences for not choosing you. If you have DV, and your prospect chooses another competitor instead, then they give up your DV and all the good things it could do for them. Every decision involves trade-offs, and trade-offs have consequences — so what are the consequences to your prospect if they make that decision?

Those consequences are the raw material to accelerate our sale and keep us out of Wimp Junction.

No Consequences?

If your prospect can decide not to do business with you, and there are *no consequences* to them if they do, then that's the right move. They are not really a prospect.

Clarity, honesty, and humility are critical to successful selling. If what you're selling doesn't have DV for this particular prospect (i.e., there are no consequences to them for not doing business with you), then the right choice is to not do business with you. This is critical to understanding (and selling on) DV.

Imagine two car dealerships next to each other. One sells upscale luxury cars with a high price tag, mostly two-seater sports cars. The other sells everyday, mainstream cars with lower price tags —

sedans, minivans, and the like. While the luxury car seller sits in their office, they can see families driving past their luxury dealership to buy sedans and minivans from the dealership next door.

Does this salesperson wring their hands and worry every time they "lose" an opportunity and someone drives off with a new minivan? Not at all — those customers weren't in the market for a luxury two-seater. No opportunity was lost — by either party.

Getting clarity around your DV allows you to target the right prospects in the marketplace, to qualify opportunities ruthlessly, and to leverage your DV so that your differentiators become must-haves in your prospect's decision-making process. You will then be in the strongest possible position to sell at high margin and avoid commoditization.

Change Hurts

Your greatest competitor in the marketplace is inertia — your prospect's option to do nothing and keep the status quo.

Prospects don't get up in the morning and say, "This is a great day to change vendors!" or, "This is a great day to issue an RFP!" or, "This is a great day to install new systems!" or, "This is a great day to overhaul our operations!"

No matter what industry you're in, no matter what you're selling, no matter what the competitive landscape might look like, the pain of change is the primary obstacle in your way.

Change is painful. In an enterprise, change is especially expensive, complicated, and risky. Someone will have to implement and oversee the change, which pulls resources away from their current priorities. Employees will have to change what they're doing and learn new processes; some might even get so frustrated that they leave, taking their talent with them. And looming over all of this is the risk that the change will be a disaster, just like that one implementation a few years ago that still gives them a headache to think about.

We often see salespeople hit the marketplace equipped with all the smart reasons — features, benefits, savings, etc. — why their prospect should change to them over their current provider. But they're rarely equipped with reasons why their prospect should change at all — and that's the first challenge they'll encounter in the marketplace, which only their Differentiating Value (DV) can answer.

To visualize the powerful effect of DV here, imagine a scale in your prospect's mind.

On one side is the pain of change; on the other side is the pain of staying the same.

Here are three key questions to ask about this scale in your prospect's mind:

Question #1: How well does your prospect believe they are doing right now, in the absence of a relationship with you?
Answer: Each person probably thinks they're doing pretty well. Even if they're already aware of and trying to fix the problem

you solve, they probably think they're making pretty good progress without you.

Question #2: How much fun is it for them to stop doing whatever they are currently doing and start doing something new with you?

Answer: About as much fun as a root canal. Humans hate change and go to great lengths to avoid it every day. On top of that, the person you're talking to may not only be comfortable with the status quo, they might have built it! They might be responsible for the patchwork mess your solution can replace. Tread carefully here; don't call their baby ugly!

We have many technology clients whose innovative solutions can replace outdated legacy systems, saving enterprises anywhere from thousands to millions of dollars each year. While it sounds like a no-brainer for the marketplace to adopt their solution, they encounter tremendous resistance from the high-ranking employees who have spent years of their career painstakingly building the patches, workarounds, and point solutions that have morphed into a Frankenstein mess that our client can replace. To endorse our client's solution would be to admit they've been doing it wrong for the last decade — and no one wants to admit that!

To make it worse, many sellers call on these prospects with an opening premise that inadvertently calls them incompetent: "We can fix the way you've been doing it wrong!" Anyone who gets a call like that will do everything in their power to make sure that seller doesn't see the light of day at their company.

This is where humility is so critical to selling. Being right, instead of being humble, will get you shown the door. Your input doesn't matter here.

In your prospect's mind, they think they're doing just fine without you. Even if "just fine" isn't perfect, it's still fine enough to stay the same and avoid going through the pain of change. When the pain of change outweighs the pain of staying the same, no sale happens.

NO SALE

This is the inertia you're up against when you're selling your solution (or even simply a concept). There are strong reasons for your prospect to maintain the status quo and avoid the costs, complexities, and risks of change. And there are even stronger reasons for some individuals in the cast of characters to resolutely defend the status quo: because they're especially at risk when change is on the horizon.

Think carefully about the message you're bringing to the marketplace in your conversations with prospects. Is it about all the wonderful things your solution could achieve for them, like lowered costs, increased savings, or faster time to market? Those are benefits — and benefits typically aren't strong enough to tilt the scale in favor of making a change.

Instead, we must ask:

Question #3: What will cause the scale to tilt in our favor, and when will it happen?

Answer: When the pain of staying the same outweighs the pain of change. That's when your sale has a chance.

SALE

As I write this manuscript, I am planning to throw a party for my father, Terry Slattery, to celebrate his upcoming anniversary of fifty years of sobriety. Fifty years without a drop of alcohol is an incredible achievement! My father went to great pains to educate me about the risks of substance abuse and alcohol addiction throughout my childhood, and one point always stood out to me: An alcoholic may hate their life with alcohol, but they won't change as long as the prospect of giving up alcohol seems more painful. The moment of hope comes when they hit rock bottom, and life with booze hurts so badly that the prospect of a life without booze — otherwise terrifying — finally looks better by comparison. That's when change has a chance.

Addiction may be an extreme example of the incredible weight of the status quo, but the same scale is in each of our heads when we face the pain of change: *We will avoid the pain of change until the pain of staying the same hurts more.*

This balance must be in the back of your mind throughout every conversation during your sale. Your prospect has every reason to avoid the pain of change *until the pain of staying the same hurts more.*

It's the law of inertia: An object at rest will stay at rest ... unless acted on by an outside force. (Spoiler alert: You will be that outside force.)

Your DV Tilts the Scale

When you do the DV exercise in the next section to determine your DV, you will drill down into your prospect's world to uncover all the problems your prospect is living with because they don't have your DV.

In short, *you will articulate the pain of staying the same.* You'll unearth the costs, consequences, and impacts of all the things your prospect is living with because they don't have your DV. You'll know what it's costing your prospect to not do business with you, how those consequences are showing up, and who's feeling them.

You'll articulate the pain of staying the same — and if that's heavier than the pain of change, then your sale has a chance.

This is why the DV exercise is so important! Sellers often focus on the good things their solution could bring to their prospects — increased savings, faster time to market, etc. — but good things don't tilt this scale! Pain tilts this scale, because pain is on both sides of it.

With the DV exercise, we dig deeply into the pain of the status quo and how it's showing up in your prospect's world. It's critical to maintain unwavering focus on your prospect: What are they living with because they don't have your DV (past, present, and future)?

That's the weight of the status quo, which will tilt the scale in your favor.

But there are two very important rules to remember about this scale:

Important Rule #1: This scale does not exist in reality. It exists in your prospect's mind! What matters is their perception, not yours.

It doesn't matter if the pain of staying the same (living with the status quo) *actually* outweighs the pain of change; what matters is your prospect's *perception* of the two pains. If they think the status quo is comfortable enough to avoid the pain of change, they will stay there. You are completely reliant on their perception.

Important Rule #2: Facts will not tilt this scale! There is nothing you can tell the prospect to tilt this scale in their mind to favor your sale.

This is because *you're not a neutral party in the conversation.* The prospect knows that your compensation is tied to your ability to drag them through the pain of change. They don't trust your motives. No matter how much they may like or trust you as a human being, they do not see you as a neutral party here.

When you speak, they don't believe you — no matter how much they may like you. Your declarations (about how bad their status quo is) will be contested. Only their own declarations about how bad the status quo is will tilt the scale in their head. But they need your help to articulate that pain.

Sell, Don't Tell

This leads us to No-Fail Selling Rule #2: Stop telling and start selling. Telling is about us and our "stuff," instead of about them (their favorite topic). Telling will not move the scale in our prospects' minds.

Terry's experience selling at IBM many years ago taught him that telling a prospect "Here's why we're different" wasn't nearly as effective as asking the prospect about the things they were likely living with in the absence of his DV.

NO-FAIL RULE #2
Stop telling and start selling.
Telling isn't selling.
Asking questions is selling.

This is key to engaging our prospects: *We don't ever explicitly tell prospects about our DV.* Rather, we leverage our DV by crafting strategic questions that will prompt the prospect to answer us and articulate the problems they're living with in the absence of our DV.

Their answers — which articulate the pain of the status quo — are what will increasingly weigh down the pain of staying the same on the scale in our prospect's mind until it finally outweighs the pain of change.

When you ask DV questions skillfully, your prospect will stop thinking about the cost of doing business with you (i.e., going through the pain of change) and start worrying about the cost of NOT doing business with you.

At Slattery, we often perform "sales autopsies" with our clients to determine what killed an opportunity. We start all the way at the beginning, asking our client exactly what their DV was for this particular opportunity. The salesperson in charge of the deal sometimes gets a little anxious or impatient here and interjects, "Yeah, but I TOLD them all about that and they STILL didn't want to move forward!" And with that, the cause of death is verified.

Telling isn't selling — asking questions is selling. Telling is a one-way ticket to Wimp Junction as we slip into Unpaid Consulting, shift the focus to us, and lose perspective on the prospect.

Throughout this book, we'll help you craft strategic questions that will help you leverage your DV and remain prospect-focused and consultative in your sales conversations.

But first, let's determine your DV.

TACTICAL

Differentiating Value (DV) creates an opportunity to alter your prospect's decision-making process so that more value is placed on your competitive strengths than on things like low prices or fees. In this section, we will share with you a powerful exercise to help you determine your DV.

When we consult with clients to help determine and articulate their DV, this exercise in corporate strategy will often fill two solid days in the C-suite. It's not easy, but it's critical.

Here we'll approach DV more from a tactical level (rather than strategic), so I don't expect you to need two days. But this chapter does require a bit of thinking on your part, so grab a pencil and paper before continuing.

Don't skip this chapter; it is the foundation for the next four stages in our Selling System to stay on the right side of the tracks at Wimp Junction.

What's Your DV?

We often open a DV session with clients with a brief explanation of DV, and then we ask them a simple question: "What's your DV?"

Their answers often focus on their strengths, like this:

> *"Our DV is accurate, trustworthy, real-time data to support decision-making."*

Naturally, when their sellers announce those strengths in the marketplace (usually with a premature pitch), their prospects inevitably answer, "Great; if we ever need that, we'll get back to you." That's because those strengths haven't yet been translated to the prospect's world. We cannot trust our prospects to do the work of translating our strengths to their world — they don't have the time, bandwidth, or experience to do it. We must do it for them.

Your DV is the translation of your unique strengths — *your differentiators* — to your prospect's world so that they *value* your differentiators over someone else's lower price in their evaluation process. That's why we call it Differentiating Value.

In order to begin the translation process, let's clarify the two flavors of DV (you'll find you have one or the other to offer the marketplace) and the critical difference between price and cost.

The Two Flavors of Differentiating Value

Differentiating Value always comes in one of two flavors. Your DV is either

+ something you have that is truly unique, like patented technology, or

+ something you can execute better, and you can prove it.

The first flavor of DV may give you a well-fortified position in the marketplace, but only for a short time. Technology will progress, patents will expire, and your competitors will catch up. Today's differentiators are tomorrow's table stakes.

Many of our high-tech clients start out with truly unique differentiators. At first, prospects are intrigued by the possibilities inherent in the hot new technology. This makes it relatively easy for sellers to get appointments with executives at their prospect organizations.

But the market catches up, often with blinding speed. Competitors begin rolling out lookalike solutions, claiming they accomplish the same things for less money. Prospects have trouble distinguishing between claims. It becomes harder for the sellers to get appointments. The unique value inherent in the hot new technology becomes table stakes to get on the RFP list.

As these changes take place, we help our clients shift their DV strategy to the second flavor — better execution — to keep their premium position in the long term.

This second flavor of DV leverages the uniqueness embedded in your business model — the way you do what you do. Other competitors may offer similar solutions, but it's the way you execute your solution that sets you apart in the marketplace. This is where some of the richest, best, longest-lasting DV is found!

We have a client — let's call them Fine Air — who sells HVAC systems for heating and cooling commercial buildings. They were early adopters of new technology that allowed them to bring precision and speed to their clients' indoor climate-control efforts. But soon, their competitors also adopted this increasingly available technology, and selling at high value became more difficult.

We helped Fine Air determine their DV in the second flavor — they had unique value embedded in their business model. They didn't just offer great HVAC systems with up-to-date technology. They also maintained an on-call staffing model that kept client support at full strength during the evenings, weekends, and holidays — which is when Murphy's Law always seemed to kick in at full strength: If something can go wrong, it will.

This meant that when a Fine Air client encountered an issue in their heating in the dead of winter on New Year's Eve, they could call Fine Air's support team, reach a human on the phone immediately, and have a technician at their building quickly. Without that quick response in the cold northern climate, water pipes could easily freeze and burst overnight, causing massive damage.

Fine Air's competitors typically followed more normal staffing flows, with full support during workday hours and lighter support during evenings, weekends, and holidays. But HVAC glitches often happen during evenings, weekends, and holidays. If a client encountered a glitch in their cooling system on July 3rd, Fine Air was on-site immediately. Their competitors might not get into the building until July 6th, when everyone was back from their long July 4th holiday weekend and the building was impossibly hot.

It didn't take long for Fine Air to dominate the market. Their mechanical systems may have been the same as their competitors' — but how they executed their business model, with intentionally heavier staffing during high-risk periods, set them apart from their competitors and allowed them to win consistently at high value.

If you find that your DV is currently of the first flavor (through superior technology or some other unique advantage), it probably won't last; it's never too early to start developing the second flavor of DV through superior execution.

Price vs. Cost

When we begin helping a client determine their DV, we find it helpful to articulate the difference between Price and Cost, or TCOOL, which is an acronym we use at Slattery for "Total Cost of Ownership Over the Life" of a product. This distinction will be useful as you go through the upcoming exercise to determine your DV — especially when you get to the third question in the exercise.

Price is the number on a price tag. Cost, however, is the full cost of ownership and includes not only the price tag but also any hidden expenses that come later. For example, two cars may have the same price tag, but if one breaks down every month while the other runs smoothly for ten years without a hiccup, then the Total Cost of Ownership Over the Life of the cars is wildly different, despite their matching price tags.

TCOOL may also include opportunity costs like lost revenues and missed strategies. For example, two machines may look alike and manufacture similar products, but the cheaper machine is out of service for an additional three hours each month for extra repairs that the more expensive machine doesn't need.

Those three hours represent lost revenues, as the company isn't manufacturing products it could have produced in that time with the more expensive machine. Those lost revenues are part of the total cost, or TCOOL, of buying the cheaper machine.

When you sell a product or service, the prospect will naturally ask you about the price of your product, so you must be cognizant of that number (especially compared to your competitors') and comfortable discussing it with prospects at the right time.

But price is only one factor of the total cost, or TCOOL, and when you're selling on value, TCOOL is the more relevant number to your sale. You will need to understand the TCOOL of your product or service, especially compared to your competitors' — because if you have Differentiating Value, you probably have a much lower TCOOL than your competitors.

Let's use an example to illustrate:

Ball Bearing, Inc. sells ball bearings for manufacturing processes. Their ball bearings are made with stronger materials than those of their competitors and last twice as long. They're also more expensive — the up-front price is higher.

Ball Bearing, Inc.'s salespeople are getting stuck at the price conversation because their prospects demand lower pricing and won't even consider buying Ball Bearing, Inc.'s version of what they think is a completely interchangeable commodity. Even when they tell prospects that their ball bearings last twice as long, the prospects still focus on price: "Yeah, but you're twice as expensive!"

To overcome the price obstacle, Ball Bearing, Inc. needs to shift the focus from Price to Cost, or TCOOL. They need to ask: "What does it really, totally cost our prospect to buy inferior ball bearings from our competitor?" That lower up-front price is only part of the story. Yes, the superior ball bearings might last twice as long as the cheaper competitors', but ... what does that really *mean* to prospects?

How much does it cost the prospect to replace those inferior ball bearings more frequently? How much revenue is lost during machine downtime when the ball bearings are getting replaced? How much do they spend in extra labor during those unnecessarily frequent replacements? How many more times a year do those replacements happen because they're not using the superior ball bearings?

This is how we translate the feature ("last twice as long") to tangible reality. Suddenly, that competitor's lower price pales next to their higher TCOOL, and Ball Bearing, Inc.'s solution looks like a steal in comparison. Their lower TCOOL is key to their Differentiating Value.

It's not enough to know that your product or service *has* a lower TCOOL — you'll actually want to run some numbers and calculate it. Rough estimates are fine, but you do want to be familiar with this part of your prospect's world so you can have an intelligent conversation with your prospect on the topic.

But (and this is very important), please remember: *You'll never tell your prospect any TCOOL number!* Don't tell them that you have a lower TCOOL than your competitors. Don't tell them how much TCOOL they're spending by not doing business with you. They will only fight you on the number. This is for your eyes only; it's critical to making you an informed participant in the conversation, but you'll never use it to club them over the head with "telling."

Note: When you're talking to prospects, you also won't use the term

TCOOL — That's a moniker we use internally to clarify that the word "cost" really includes total long-term fees, charges, missed revenues, and built-in expenses over the life of a product, and is different from "price." When you engage your prospects, you'll simply use the words "price" and "cost."

THE EXERCISE: *Three Questions*
Now that we've clarified the two flavors of DV and the difference between price and TCOOL, let's begin to determine and articulate your DV by answering three questions. (Grab that paper and pencil!)

Question #1: What do you offer that is either truly unique (e.g., patented technology) or executed better than your competitors?

Remember, there are two flavors of DV: Either *what* you offer is unique, or *how* you offer it is better (and you can prove it). This question is all about you, so you can talk about your strengths, features, and benefits here.

Let me use an example to illustrate:

> *"Our DV is accurate, trustworthy, real-time data to support decision-making."*

There are three features there:
1. Accurate data
2. Trustworthy data
3. Real-time data

If we were doing this exercise in person, I'd ask our client to elaborate what they mean by each of those features — are they patent-protected? Or are they executed better than the competition?

This is important: The "better execution" strengths are often *hidden in your business model* with that second flavor of DV. How your business operates, compared to your competitors', is probably where some of your unique strengths lie.

For example, those data solutions might not be proprietary or patent-protected, but perhaps the company uniquely maintains 24/7 on-site support staff at their data center, and this ensures less downtime (and, thus, more real-time data) than their daytime-only competitors. That round-the-clock staffing is a unique strength.

Here is what our example might look like if we expanded our answers:

1. *Accurate data* = We sweep a wider sample of information, making our data more accurate than our competitors'.
2. *Trustworthy data* = We source our data from more reliable banks of information, so our data is more trustworthy than our competitors'.
3. *Real-time data* = We maintain 24/7 onsite support staff at the data center, which ensures our data is more up-to-date than our competitors', whose processing is delayed by downtime.

So to answer this first question, start by listing the top three strengths you offer. They might be related to your product quality, time to market, customer support ... anything you see as your top unique strengths in the marketplace.

1. _____

2. _____

3. _____

Now, read your list again. Can your competitors say, "Me too"? If so, then we must ask: Are these differentiators you've listed truly unique?

Some of the strengths that are often listed here, like great service, wonderful people, responsiveness, and great technology, are simply table stakes for the RFP list. So ask yourself if each item you listed above is, in fact, unique; if it is, then leave it on the list. But if it isn't, then remove it. (I recommend moving it over to a list called Table Stakes and keeping it there as a reminder that, while necessary, it's not DV, and we definitely shouldn't be talking about it with prospects.)

At this step, it's critical to separate out the truly unique from the table stakes. Salespeople often enter the marketplace talking about the same features and benefits that all their competitors are touting. Sounding exactly like your competitors is a one-way ticket to Wimp Junction.

With this exercise, we're weeding out all the common language you share with your competitors and leaving only those things that are truly unique to your solution and the way you do business.

Now, this is a great list — but it is not your DV yet! Too many people stop here. Too often, salespeople take this list, run into the marketplace, rattle off their unique strengths, and expect that the prospect knows exactly what each strength means for them. They don't! They need your help translating it to their world.

That's why we move on to Question #2.

Question #2: What are all the consequences — to the prospect — in the absence of each strength you listed? What happens to your prospect if they don't have each strength you listed above?

We're asking you to detail the negative consequences to your prospect in the *absence* of each of your strengths. It's a little counterintuitive.

When we run this exercise with clients, salespeople often want to answer the opposite, positive question instead: What good things will happen to the prospect if they HAVE each of our strengths? Unfortunately, the positive angle is not adequately helpful. In general, people move more quickly to avoid a pain than they do to achieve a pleasure. Benefits, benefits, and more benefits won't move the needle for your sale. We're weaving a picture of what life WITHOUT your DV looks like for your prospect.

Remember, the foundation of DV is the simple rule from Economics 101: There are no free moves. Every decision involves trade-offs, and trade-offs have consequences. *What are the consequences to your prospect because they don't have your DV at work for them?*

Your answers will begin to articulate the costs and pain of the status quo, which must ultimately outweigh the pain of change for your sale to succeed.

So, to answer Question #2 here, start with the list of strengths you created from Question #1 and answer: What are all the consequences — to the prospect's enterprise — in the absence of each strength you listed?

Consequences of not having Strength #1:

_____

_____

Consequences of not having Strength #2:

_____

_____

Consequences of not having Strength #3:

_____

_____

The more specific your answers are, the better!

To continue our example above, this is what our first strength, accurate data, might look like when we expand it with the consequences to our prospect in the absence of it:

Without our version of accurate data (swept from wider samples): *"Our prospects' strategic decisions are made based on inaccurate data pulled from a narrower sample of information."*

Do you see how this answer begins drawing out the consequences that are happening to the prospect in the absence of that strength? *They're making strategic decisions based on inaccurate data.* We're filling in our answers with some language that gets us closer to the prospect's world.

But we're not done yet; we must go deeper still into the prospect's world to translate the concepts above (still just concepts!) to the daily reality of what the prospect is truly living with in the absence of our DV.

The real translation, and the hardest work, happens with Question #3.

Question #3: What is the impact of each consequence? In other words, "So what?" You wrote down some consequences when you answered Question #2. But ... so what?

In this most difficult step, you must answer the "So what?" question in great detail. It is not easy! You are donning a hard hat, picking up your shovel, and digging deep into the DV mine for nuggets of gold.

Here are some questions to help you dig:
 * What's happening to whom because this DV component has not been adequately valued?
 * How has it shown up? (That's past-tense pain.)
 * How is it showing up right now? (That's present-tense pain.)
 * How will it show up? (That's future-tense pain.)
 * What are all the other impacts across the enterprise?
 * What metrics do they use to measure those impacts?

- Whose dashboard is showing red in those metrics?
- Who's paying for this problem?
- Who's doing workarounds because of it?

Think in terms of TCOOL — the total cost of ownership over the life of this product or service. If your prospect doesn't buy from you, and they go with a competitor instead, what costs will they incur for another decade? What opportunities will they miss out on because they don't have your DV at work for them?

At this step, people often skirt the work of digging in altogether, and they jump up to a 30,000-foot view by trying to lump all the problems together into a single "silver bullet" summary that applies to everyone, everywhere.

To continue our example above using accurate data as a unique differentiator, a silver-bullet answer here in Step 3 might sound like this:

> *"Without our version of accurate data, our prospects will make strategic decisions based on inaccurate data ... and that means ...* they'll make poor strategic decisions and lose money!*"*

This is a useless effort! The phrase "make poor strategic decisions" will not resonate with your prospects. You'll never use it in the marketplace. We're not writing a business school paper where brevity or intellectual crispness will get you an A. This is the marketplace, where you must be finely tuned to your prospect's world — their struggles, their costs, their pains, and all the things they're currently living with because they're not your customer. Do not craft a nice, bland, vague, intellectual summary. Dig into the dirt.

At this step, the goal is to INCREASE the amount of text on your page, NOT reduce it to a summary. We're looking for details, rawness, honesty, real-life tedium, daily annoyances, missed opportunities, bleeding money, emergency meetings, burdensome workarounds, and TCOOL.

So, at this step, take each item on its own (like "accurate data") and focus on it by answering what we call the Cinnamon Question, based on a book my father, Terry Slattery, wrote on DV called *The Cinnamon Story*.

The Cinnamon Question is this: "What's happening to *whom* in the absence of your DV?" (It's simply a more eloquent way of asking, "So what?")

Let's continue our example DV, using "accurate data" to show how we dig for gold:

When we answered Question #1, we determined that our unique strength was: *Accurate data, because we sweep a wider sample of data, making our data more accurate than our competitors'.*

And when we answered Question #2, we determined that, as a consequence of not having our unique version of accurate data, *prospects were making strategic decisions based on inaccurate data.*

Now, in Question #3, we answer: *What's happening to whom as a result of that?* In other words: They're coming to the wrong conclusions ... SO WHAT?

Here are some possibilities:

> *When the prospects make strategic decisions based on inaccurate data, they may invest money in directives to solve problems that the data seemed to indicate exist but which don't actually exist. If they had accurate data, they'd be able to avoid wasting money on poor investments, and they'd be able to invest in solving their true problems instead.*

But we don't stop there!

We keep digging by asking, "So what?" So the prospects pour money into bad strategic initiatives ... so what? What do those bad strategic initiatives look like? What are they costing the enterprise? Who gets the financial bill for them? Who else cares about this? What metrics are showing red on their dashboards? Who is doing workarounds because of this? Answer each question here — not just one or two!

- What are the consequences of that? *Because they're pouring money into bad strategic initiatives, they're unable to invest in solving their true problems instead.*
- So what? *So ... their true unsolved problems continue to plague them.*
- Who is doing workarounds? *Operations; those who are still living with the real unsolved problems.*
- So what? *Ops is probably seeing increasingly fast churn as people get disgruntled and leave, and they're having trouble refilling positions.*
- What are they costing the enterprise? *The true unsolved problems are probably costing about a million dollars a year. That doesn't count paying people to do extra workarounds or the churn on payroll.*

- And how much are those costing the enterprise? *Easily five million dollars a year.*
- Who gets the financial bill for them? *The CFO, and ultimately, the CEO.*
- Who else cares about this? *Probably the Chief Strategy Officer, who can't pursue strategic initiatives because the enterprise is too busy pouring money into bad investments, and ultimately the board, whose reputation is tied to their ability to pursue the right strategic initiatives for growth.*
- What metrics are showing red on their dashboard? *Time; delayed strategic initiatives.*
- And how does that manifest in the organization? *They're falling behind their competitors who are solving these problems faster and more efficiently.*

Now THIS is gold: Your prospect is falling behind their competitors because they aren't solving the right problems. (The CSO will be your friend here!) Your prospect is also bleeding money while they try to solve the wrong problems, losing quality employees they can't replace, and dealing with an increasingly disgruntled team culture.

This language is getting to the root of it and is rich fodder for conversations. And this is just a high-level first pass! Imagine how much richer our material will be when we spend a few hours thinking this through.

When we started this exercise, "accurate data" was just one strength that we rattled off quickly in a list that was totally focused on us: "Our DV is accurate, trustworthy, real-time data to support decision-making."

If we called on a prospect and told them, "We offer accurate data," no prospect would ever jump to a conclusion like this: "Ah! Thank goodness you're calling me — my Operations team has been buried for eighteen months under senseless projects we've been pouring money into while we try to fix the underlying problems we can't quite identify because we've been making inaccurate conclusions, all because we're procuring our data from a less accurate source than you!"

It's too far of a stretch — they can't connect your strengths to the consequences they're currently living with in the absence of your DV. *You're the seller — that's your job.*

Notice that all of this effort so far has been dedicated to just the first of three unique strengths we identified in Question #1: accurate, trustworthy, real-time data. To complete this step, we would run this exact same extraction for the "trustworthy" and "real-time" strengths as well.

So, to complete Step #3, take each of the unique strengths you wrote in Step #1 along with the consequences you detailed for each in Step #2 and now elaborate on each consequence by writing out (in detail!) exactly what's happening to whom in the absence of your DV. And don't stop there! Keep digging by asking, "So what?" "So what?" "So what?"

What is each consequence costing the enterprise? Who gets the financial bill for them? Whose dashboard is showing red because of them? How are they showing up elsewhere in the organization? Who is doing workarounds to accommodate them? The more specific your answers are, the better!

◆ What's happening to whom because of the consequences of not having Strength #1?

_____

_____

_____

_____

◆ What's happening to whom because of the consequences of not having Strength #2?

_____

_____

_____

_____

◆ What's happening to whom because of the consequences of not having Strength #3?

_____

_____

When you're answering, think about all three time tenses: past, present, and future.

◆ What's *been happening* to whom because they haven't been your customer?

◆ What's *happening* to whom right now because they're not your customer?

◆ What's *going to happen* to whom because they're still not your customer?

(Don't worry if you find it easier to unearth more future-tense pain than past-tense pain or vice versa. Some of our clients, such as those in the insurance sector, rely entirely on future-tense pain, as they mitigate future risk. Others rescue their prospects after they've built up a lot of past-tense pain. Your list will be unique to you. The goal here is to brainstorm a LOT of text.)

This isn't easy; it's hard work. But it is critically important work. We're translating the marketing message focused on us to a selling-ready language focused on the *prospect* to equip us for the Last Mile of selling. And since we are completely dependent on the prospect's consent and cooperation to move forward at every step in our sale, our focus must necessarily be on them; we must know and understand their world intimately.

The gold nuggets you unearth in your digging here are the words and phrases that encapsulate your prospect's pain and frustrations. They are the material you will use when crafting strategic questions to engage your prospect in conversation. Since they're completely focused on the prospect, you'll be less likely to trip your prospect's "sales tripwire" (usually triggered by a premature pitch) and more likely to win their cooperation (since you'll be genuinely focused on them).

You'll also be more likely to be seen as a consultative seller, since you'll have an understanding of their world that very few of your competitors will go to the effort to uncover. And you'll get all of it done without doing any Unpaid Consulting.

We recommend doing this exercise deeply and thoroughly from start to finish. This will produce excellent language that translates your unique DV to your prospect's world, which you can use again and again in your sales. We also recommend refreshing your answers every time you pursue an important competitive sale or encounter a new type of prospect; the effort will unearth the unique consequences experienced by the particular prospect you're targeting, and you'll develop laser-focused language that resonates with them. We also recommend refreshing your answers at least annually as the marketplace landscape changes and competitors catch up; you may even find your DV shifting from the first to second flavor with time. We'll talk more about this in Chapter 10. Refreshing your DV will keep your language relevant and prospect-centric as you pursue your sales.

Common Issues

Having done this exercise thousands of times with thousands of companies and even more salespeople, we are familiar with a few common issues that arise when clients do it for the first time.

At first pass, our clients often try to complete this exercise as if they're writing it for a business school paper; their answers are clean, crisp, intellectual, and logical.

Here's what it might sound like:

"Because our prospect doesn't have our DV, they are facing ..."
- *"higher employee turnover"*
- *"challenges when filling open positions"*
- *"increased payroll expenses"*

These answers are too neat and sterile. These are facts, and they are accurate facts — but they're not quite the rich gold nuggets we're looking for. They're a symptom of jumping up to that 30,000-foot view, where we try to encapsulate all our prospects' problems into a single easy-to-use summary.

So to counter this tendency, I often tell our clients to check their work against three litmus tests to ensure they're on the right track during this exercise:

LITMUS TEST #1
How much text have you written
in your answers to each question?

If you have an *increasing* amount of text as you go from Question #1 to Question #2 and Question #3 (especially at Question #3!), then you're on the right track. If, however, you've reverted to brief and intellectual answers at Question #3, then you're not going deep enough.

If you don't yet have an abundance of text in your answers to Question #3 (more than you had at #2 and #1), then simply ask "So what?" a few more times and resist that ever-present temptation to jump up to 30,000 feet. The silver-bullet summary may feel good to write but is utterly useless in the marketplace. Your prospects won't be converted by bumper-sticker brevity, no matter how impatient they may seem. You'll be pursuing your sale over many months of outreach, engagement, and conversations; you need a LOT more prospect-centric language than just a pithy headline.

The goal is to have more text in your answers to Question #3 than you had at #2, and more there than you had at #1. Let your pen flow freely!

LITMUS TEST #2
What language do you use
in your answers to each question?

Imagine your ideal prospect coming home at the end of a long day. They're exhausted and they're frustrated because they spent all day handling the messes your DV could solve (but they don't know about you yet). They've been dealing with the problems, sitting in emergency meetings, putting out fires, bleeding money, funding workarounds. They walk in, hunched over and scowling. They head to the sink, blast some cold water into a tall glass, chug it down it in two gulps, and then turn, red-faced, to their beloved spouse, and vent:

> *"Spouse, let me tell you, I have had it* UP TO HERE. *Work is driving me absolutely crazy! I'm dealing with"* — and they draw in their breath, winding up to tell their beloved spouse exactly what they navigated today — *"challenges when filling open positions."*

Do you see how that language is just too sterile? No one talks in corporate language when they're venting to their spouse about all the problems they're living with at work.

Human beings make decisions on emotion and justify them later. If you're trying to meet your prospect in their pain and help them out of it, but your language is dry, intellectual, and business-school crisp, even rational, you won't resonate with them because you are not speaking to their emotions. You need specific, real-life language here.

Run a quick check of your sales assets. If your outreach messages have dry phrases, like "higher employee turnover" or "increased expenditures," this is a symptom of not going deep enough in Step #3.

In this exercise, our result should be language that's a realistic reflection of all the things your prospect is living with because they're not your customer. If you have intellectual language here in Step #3, go deeper and translate it to the real-life challenges your prospect is facing daily (with nitty-gritty detail!) because they're not your customer.

LITMUS TEST #3
Who is listed in your answers to each question?

In a complex sale, you will encounter various players in the cast of characters at your prospect enterprise. When doing this DV exercise, your answers to Question #3 should be so specific that you're naming actual roles and titles of people who are affected by the consequences of not having your DV at the enterprise.

Remember, the Cinnamon Question asks: What's happening to *whom* because their enterprise is not your customer?

An answer that's too vague might be: "They're having trouble filling open positions." Who's "they"? Who's having trouble — the enterprise? The CEO? Operations? HR? The third junior assistant staffing coordinator? And how is this showing up in their life?

Properly filled out, you might have an answer that sounds like this:

> *"The* Operations *team is having trouble filling open positions, which leaves critical processes unfinished in IT security ... which makes the* COO's *life a living hell because they have to report every security breach to the* board, *and they're getting tired of standing in front of the board to get yelled at for another breach every other month. It also leaves the* VP of Talent *in a mess because they look like they're ineffective at the recruiting side of their job, even though they're probably working overtime to compensate for the awful recruiting software they're stuck with."*

Dive into your prospect's world with this exercise, and let your pen flow freely. Once you have passed all three litmus tests — that is, once you have written extensively about your prospect's problems, from their perspective and in their language, and you have identified all the players in your sale's cast of characters — then congratulations! You made it through the DV exercise!

You now have enhanced clarity around those components of your DV that will bring your prospects maximum value. Over the course of your sale, you will drive these DV components into the "must have" category in your prospect's evaluation and decision-making processes so they value your differentiators over someone else's lower price.

Naturally, you won't ever tell your prospects about your DV. Telling is about us; questioning is about them. So you will craft strategic questions that leverage your DV to open up your prospect's awareness that things could be different or better. The language you teased out of the above exercise will become the meat of those strategic questions and will keep you from being commoditized at Wimp Junction.

When you completed this DV exercise, you proactively uncovered one of the most valuable pieces of intelligence that will speed up the cadence of your sale and get your value recognized earlier: the identity of your true prospecting target.

Let's concentrate on them next.

CHAPTER FIVE

Target

The Prospect's Buying System		Your System

STEP 1
The prospect lies to the salesperson.

STAGE 1
Differentiate

STEP 2
The prospect gets the salesperson to provide valuable information and a quote.

STAGE 2
Target

STAGE 3
Engage

STEP 3
The prospect lies about what's going to happen next.

STAGE 4
Commit

STEP 4
The prospect doesn't answer or return the salesperson's calls.

STAGE 5
Secure

WIMP JUNCTION®

STRATEGIC

There's rarely a single decision-maker in complex sales. You will usually have to contend with multiple stakeholders at your prospect organization, and they'll have competing agendas with vastly different priorities. Some of them may even be hostile to your solution because it's a threat to their world.

Differentiating Value enhances your ability to strategically target the right prospects, more quickly navigate the full cast of characters at your prospect enterprise, and accelerate the cadence of your sale.

Remember, there are no free moves. If you have DV, then someone, somewhere at your prospect organization is paying right now for not having it — even though they don't know about you.

From the DV exercise you completed in the previous chapter, let's look at your answers to Question #3: What's happening to whom at your prospect enterprise because they're not your customer?

The titles and roles listed in your DV answers reveal the identity of the real strategic target of your selling efforts: your Emotional Customer.

Your Real Target

At Slattery, we refer to two kinds of customers in the cast of characters at your prospect organization: the Logical Customer and the Emotional Customer.

These titles do not refer to the way this person may think or behave! Rather, the titles help us remember the distinct features of these two very different people:

The Logical Customer is a person at your prospect organization who has an intellectual, logical relationship with the problem you're out to solve — not a visceral, emotional relationship with the problem. In other words, they're not living with the painful day-to-day consequences of not being your customer. They're often targeted by sellers because they seem to be a logical starting point for the sale. (They're also likely to be the person targeting your company with an RFP or RFQ.)

The Emotional Customer, on the other hand, is a person at your prospect organization who feels the pain and consequences of not having your Differentiating Value in their life. That's why they're called the "Emotional" Customer — they are feeling the pain (the strongest driver of human emotion and behavior) and venting to their spouse at night about the problem you solve and how it impacts them on a daily basis. However, they probably don't know or care that you exist. They're often not targeted or included in early discussions (though excluding them is a mistake).

Let's explore the deeper characteristics, tendencies, and motivations of each of these two players.

The Logical Customer

The Logical Customer tends to be:

- Easy to find (and every competitor has already found and targeted them)
- Hard to close
- Paid to talk to salespeople
- Price sensitive
- Interested in not changing; invested in perpetuating the status quo
- Isolated from the consequences of not changing
- Bearing much of the pain of change
- At risk if the change is not successful

- Accruing few or no rewards if the change is successful
- Measured by limited performance metrics, usually related to "How much juice did you squeeze from the vendor?"
- Isolated from the consequences of delay or of undervaluing your DV (they don't care how long it takes to solve the problem because it's ultimately someone else's problem)

Logical Customers are often found in Purchasing, Vendor Management, Information Technology, and Supply Chain Management. In your sale, however, they might be somewhere else; the identities of the Logical and Emotional Customers depend on the unique DV you bring to that opportunity.

Because they're price sensitive and invested in the status quo, the Logical Customer will probably try to pull you down to their side of the tracks at Wimp Junction. If the Logical Customer is your primary target in your prospecting efforts and your conversations, then you're likely experiencing unnecessary slowdowns in your sale.

Logical Customers' Lies at Wimp Junction

Logical Customers are the consummate buyers who will lie about their authority, timeline, and intentions in order to pull you down to their side of the buying tracks at Wimp Junction.

They'll lie about their authority by saying, "I'm the decision-maker." This lie traps and isolates hopeful salespeople at Wimp Junction who think they've made it to their final destination. They settle in, get comfortable, and invest their time and resources with this one person who they think will ultimately get their sale over the finish line. (Lots of demos happen here!)

Of course, there is never just one decision-maker in a complex sale, and asking who will make the decision does not a sale make. The salesperson who believes the Logical Customer's lie about their identity as a decision-maker, and fails to ask how the decision will be made, thus fails to expand the cast of characters to include more strategic targets who might actually want the problem fixed and the benefits flowing to the organization.

With this simple lie about their authority, the Logical Customer can sequester the salesperson and avoid the risk of someone else in the organization overriding their delays and deciding, "Yes, we DO need this solution!"

Logical Customers may also lie about their timeline; it's not uncommon for a Logical Customer to appear to be in a massive hurry: "We need something up and running in ninety days — can we get a proposal by next week at the latest?" The urgency often causes salespeople, excited by the imminent built-in closing date, to rush to provide valuable information and a quote without asking deeper questions to qualify the opportunity, like, "What's going on in your world that's causing this to be a fire?"

If the salesperson simply asked a few good questions to qualify the opportunity before believing the prospect's rush, they'd often find that not only is there a lack of real urgency, there's often a lack of any powerful motivation to change at all. The lie is simply a ploy to get the salesperson to provide valuable information and a quote without asking too many questions (Step 2 at Wimp Junction). The Logical Customer collects the information, lies to the salesperson about what will happen next (Step 3 at Wimp Junction), and goes dark.

Finally, Logical Customers lie about their intentions by saying, "I'm interested." The salesperson who believes this lie fails to validate whether or not there really is any motivation to change at the organization; they simply move forward with Unpaid Consulting by providing valuable information and a quote (Step 2 at Wimp Junction).

This interest may be feigned, or it might be genuine but academic — in other words, the Logical Customer is interested in the information the salesperson can provide them for free, but they're NOT interested in making a change. They have other motives for collecting information from salespeople.

With the valuable information provided by the salesperson, the Logical Customer can drive a harder bargain with their incumbent provider in an upcoming contract renewal. Thus, they'll avoid going through a change and will probably even get recognized at their organization for the paltry savings, despite perpetuating the problem.

The Logical Customer may also exploit the salesperson's valuable information to construct their own internal solution, again avoiding the pain of change. Even if their DIY solution is complicated, expensive, and ineffective, they'll probably get kudos internally for the build.

The Logical Customer may also happily augment their PhD dissertation with the most up-to-date industry and technology information the salesperson provides. This may sound ridiculous, but in high-tech spaces, it isn't uncommon to see Logical Customers working toward their advanced degrees on the side; they are eager to absorb information from salespeople who often bring the latest advancements and innovations to the marketplace.

Finally, the Logical Customer may simply plunk the salesperson's valuable information onto a spreadsheet, where all solutions look alike, as they prepare to issue an RFP. If this Logical Customer is allowed to run the RFP, then lowest price will ultimately be the deciding factor in their decision (if they ever make one at all). Remember, the RFP is a luau, and the Logical Customer is looking for a pig.

No Teaching

No-Fail Selling Rule #3 says this: Sell to prospects; teach customers. Do not assume that in order to help your prospect understand your DV, you must teach them until they "get it." Logical Customers want you to do this so they can collect valuable information through your Unpaid Consulting.

NO-FAIL RULE #3
Sell to prospects; teach customers.

But selling and teaching are two very different things. You can sell consultatively and remain laser-focused on the prospect and their world through the strategic questions you ask (we will teach you exactly how to do this in Chapter 7). But teaching is premature.

Teaching is about us and our solution. It's perfectly fine to be a valuable teaching resource for your paying customers. But you, the seller, have limited time and resources to spend in the marketplace, and teaching prospects about you and your solution will land you squarely on the Logical Customer's side of the tracks at Wimp Junction as you provide Unpaid Consulting. Teaching will also alienate the prospects who didn't ask you to teach them anything (don't jump into a premature pitch!). Prospects hate getting presentations they didn't request.

We coach many brilliant Subject-Matter Experts (SMEs) who must sell their high-tech solution to prospects in the marketplace. It's a difficult shift for them to make from teaching prospects about the solution (which they love to do!) to selling their DV instead (which requires a much more prospect-centric focus). But once they make that shift, they find themselves closing more opportunities in less time at higher value because they no longer get stuck at Wimp Junction with super-interested Logical Customers (often fellow SMEs).

Save the teaching efforts for your paying customers, and focus on selling instead.

The Emotional Customer

After our clients realize they've been talking to Logical Customers who slow the cadence of their opportunities to a screeching halt, we turn our attention to the work they've done on their Differentiating Value to identify their real targets: the Emotional Customers.

Our clients answer the Cinnamon Question: "What's happening to whom at our prospect organization because they're not our customer?"

The result of their work, after digging into the question and answering it thoroughly, is a list of titles in the cast of characters who are living with the consequences of not having their DV: the Emotional Customers.

The Emotional Customer tends to be:

* Hard to find
* Easy to close
* Baffled as to why you're calling them
* Experiencing the consequences of not doing business with you
* Getting the bill for those consequences
* Utterly uninterested in your "stuff" (and will send you to the Logical Customer if you talk about it)
* In a position to tell the Logical Customer what to do

What really endears the Emotional Customer to us is the fact that they can usually tell the Logical Customer what to do. It's an easy litmus test to check your cast of characters: If you think you're talking to the Emotional Customer because they seem "emotionally" invested in getting this solution implemented, but their title is Third Assistant Junior Controller, they don't have enough authority to get you into the company cafeteria, let alone get your sale over the finish line. They're not your Emotional Customer.

Remember No-Fail Selling Rule #1: There are no free moves. If you really have Differentiating Value, then someone somewhere in your prospect organization is paying for not having it. That someone is your Emotional Customer.

The cost of the problem and the cost of delay are the Emotional Customer's expediters. They can crush the Logical Customer's delaying and lying.

Finding your Emotional Customers

To find your Emotional Customers, answer the Cinnamon Question: What's happening *to whom* at your prospect organization because they are not your customer? Expand your answer to include all the consequences they're experiencing because they're not your customer: past, present, and future. What consequences has your prospect organization been living with because they didn't have your DV? On top of that, what consequences are they living with right now because they don't have your DV? And on top of that, what consequences will they experience in the future if they don't have your DV?

Think strategically — what ground have they already lost to their competitors because they didn't have your DV? What opportunities can't they take advantage of right now because they don't have your DV? What strategies will they not be able to accomplish if they don't have your DV in the future?

Do you see how these questions in all three tenses (past, present, and future) help to pile up the strategic pain and consequences of not having your DV? We're beyond any feature-and-benefits presentation here; we're thinking and flying at C-suite altitudes.

Follow each pain nerve as high as you possibly can in the organization, like tracing a nerve up the arm from the finger to the shoulder. This will help you target the highest-ranking (and most influential) Emotional Customers.

Case Study: *Billing*

To illustrate the powerful acceleration that can happen when you shift from targeting Logical Customers to targeting Emotional Customers, let's examine the case of one of our clients at Slattery — we'll call them Billing Technologies. Billing Technologies sells solutions to hospitals to expedite patient billing, helping the hospital collect more money up front and prevent past-due accounts.

The integration of their suite of solutions delivers a higher level of return on investment faster than the industry has ever seen.

Before we started working together, Billing Technologies regularly began their sales by targeting VPs of Revenue Cycle Management (RCM); they found themselves with increasingly long sales cycles and tremendous pressure to prove their solution with endless demos.

A VP of Revenue Cycle Management sounded like a logical target. It was, in fact, a Logical Customer: they would bear all the pain of change when implementing a new solution (they may even have to fire team members who are manually working outdated collections processes); their internal brand with the organization would fare poorly if the new system didn't do what the seller promised (they've seen that before!); and they probably wouldn't be recognized in the event it were to succeed because the benefits will accrue elsewhere in the organization (as the money received up front would avoid RCM altogether and flow straight to Finance's Profit and Loss statement).

These Logical Customers had nothing to lose by taking months to meander through endless demos from various technology providers. They saw the benefit of the solution but couldn't overcome (or even articulate) their own reluctance to go through the change. Meanwhile, the hospital's head of Finance had no idea that they were unnecessarily bleeding millions of dollars every month because the hospital continued to operate under outdated manual billing processes, let alone that the bleeding could be stopped.

We helped Billing Technologies target the Chief Financial Officer instead, using the right strategic questions to open an awareness of everything the CFO was living with because they didn't have our client's DV in their organization. (This Emotional Customer was, of course, just one of multiple different Emotional Customers in the cast of characters.) The CFO wanted the unnecessary spend solved now. Sales cycles shrank because the Logical Customer was no longer allowed to take a two-year "walk in the park" getting demos and pondering proposals.

For our clients, this tends to be an aha moment when we're working together. They realize that they've been targeting and interacting with Logical Customers, who have absolutely zero interest in making a change.

Proactive vs. Reactive Targeting

When we begin working with new clients through their pipeline of sales opportunities in progress, they often debrief us on calls they've recently had with various stakeholders at their prospect organizations. (If they're really new to working with us, they might debrief us on calls they've recently had with various self-proclaimed decision-makers.)

In those meetings, we always ask the salesperson a very important question: Were you talking with the Logical Customer or the Emotional Customer?

A moment passes; they look off into the distance, thinking about it, and finally answer with a nod: "The Emotional Customer — they were definitely emotionally tied to getting this problem solved."

That's what we call "reactive targeting," and it's fraught with risk. Logical Customers are consummate liars about their authority and intent, and they do a great impression of needing a particular pain solved NOW. It's a ploy to pull salespeople to Step #2 of their buying system, providing valuable information and a quote.

(Even if they're good human beings who aren't consciously trying to lie to you, and they are genuinely interested in what you sell for academic reasons, they honestly don't have any intent to make a change, at all. They're Logical Customers — they're invested in the status quo. Your opportunity will die in their office.)

Reactive targeting also carries the risk that the salesperson might not only misread but misappropriate the characteristics of the Logical and Emotional customers. I've heard salespeople conclude, "They seem like a pretty logical person, so they must be the Logical Customer." Nothing could be further from the truth; remember, these titles do not refer to how the person thinks or behaves. Rather, they refer to the person's relationship to the problem: Are they an intellectual observer to the problem (Logical Customer), or someone who is feeling the pain of having the problem (Emotional Customer)?

Reactive targeting takes a long time to accomplish too; you'll need to have a lot of conversations with various stakeholders, scratching your head after each one to figure out whether the person you just talked to was an Emotional or Logical Customer, checking each person against our list of Attributes every time.

Proactive targeting, on the other hand, is when you take your DV work and proactively, strategically, determine who your Emotional Customers will be. They're the ones who are funding the problem you can solve. It takes some homework, but it is overall faster and far more effective at finding your Emotional Customers than reactive targeting.

To target proactively, think broadly, across your entire prospect organization — the Emotional Customer will often be in a completely different business unit, far from the Logical Customer you may have been targeting until now. This distance is called isolation.

Isolation

Isolation is the distance between a decision and its consequences. Isolation is always present in a complex sale.

Isolation allows one stakeholder (usually the Logical Customer) to make a decision and remain isolated from the costs or consequences of that decision. The costs and consequences of their decision accrue to another part of the enterprise, where another stakeholder (usually the Emotional Customer) feels them.

If you have DV, then your prospect enterprise is accruing costs and consequences of not doing business with you — but those costs and consequences are not felt equally across the organization. The person who's funding that problem (the Emotional Customer) doesn't know about you and your solution. The person who's invested in the status quo (the Logical Customer) is isolated from the costs and consequences of continuing the status quo.

Isolation is quicksand in the landscape of a complex sale. Your Logical Customer may choose to drag out your sale, trying to squeeze a few more concessions out of you. They don't care if it takes another six months to evaluate your solution because they remain isolated from the costs and consequences of that delay, which are accruing daily to the Emotional Customer in another part of the organization.

Your Emotional Customer may be vexed by the problems that show up on their dashboards, but they don't have the perspective or experience to connect the dots to the source of the problem. Your selling efforts will help your Emotional Customer connect those dots and overcome isolation.

(Incidentally, this is another reason why human sellers are so important for that Last Mile of selling — only a human can identify, navigate, and overcome the phenomenon of isolation at a prospect enterprise!)

As a seller, you must be aware of isolation and attempt to overcome it by connecting the decisions made by Logical Customers to the consequences felt by the Emotional Customers. When a Logical Customer tells you they need to sit on this idea for a few more months and think about possibly considering making a change, you can ask them: "And who absorbs the costs while you're waiting?"

Multiple Channels in the Cast of Characters

In a complex sale, you will probably have multiple Logical Customers and multiple Emotional Customers. It is critically important to open as many channels of communication as you can at your prospect enterprise. Complex sales can take a long time, and it's possible to lose contacts as they change jobs or retire. You don't want to be approaching the finish line after twelve months of work only to get stuck starting over at square one upon your single channel's unexpected retirement, medical leave, reorganization, firing, relocation, or death.

We recommend our clients open at least six channels of communication at their prospect organization. You want at least two or three solid Emotional Customers, and another two or three people who can be your coaches or champions as you navigate the cast of characters.

Coaches are people inside the prospect organization who may not be part of the decision-making process but can help coach you on navigating the org chart; an example might be an Executive Assistant who answers your cold call and points you to other stakeholders in the cast of characters. Or maybe it's someone you already know in another business unit who can help introduce you to your Emotional Customers.

Similarly, your champions won't be voting on your solution but will work enthusiastically to influence the decision-making process in your favor; they can come from anywhere in the organization, like a mid-level Director you met at a conference who's willing to stick their neck out to get this problem solved. They're probably feeling some of the pain radiating from the problem, but don't have enough elevation to fix it. Their support will help your case nonetheless.

You'll have to interact with the Logical Customer, too, and that's fine — your strategy will be to pull the Emotional Customer's agenda in to every conversation with the Logical Customer so the full cost of the problem remains front and center. You'll also maintain situational awareness so they don't pull you down to their side of the tracks at Wimp Junction.

Economic Democracy

In every enterprise, there are more requests for funds than there are funds available. Your solution isn't simply competing against other similar solutions in the marketplace; it's also up against your prospect organization's potential investments in a freshly-paved parking lot, new hires, higher insurance costs, upgraded software, and more. These competing priorities all have their advocates within the organization.

The way your prospect organization reconciles these issues often resembles an economic democracy: Every dollar's worth of pain equals one vote. The person with the most dollars at stake gets the most votes.

For example, let's say you manufacture medical device components at a company called Exact Components, Inc. You sell these components to major medical device companies. Your components are very similar to your competitors', but your DV lies in the execution of your business processes: You can help your major clients get a new high-quality device to market about two months faster than your competitors.

Your competitors, however, charge a significantly smaller up-front price, and the Logical Customer in Procurement cares deeply about getting the lowest possible price for what appears to be totally interchangeable commodity components. No matter how interested they may appear in Exact Components, Inc.'s solution, they do not care about anything other than lowest price. If your solution costs one million dollars more than your competitor's, then this Logical Customer will be equipped with 1,000,000 votes against you in the economic democracy. If up-front price is the only number on the table, you'll lose.

But since your DV can help the medical device company get to market faster, then one of your Emotional Customers will be the one *who owns device launch strategy*. This person will feel the pain and consequences of a two-month delay getting a new medical device to market and losing precious market share to more nimble competitors. This person will be reporting lower-than-forecasted revenue numbers to the Board every month for the next three years. That two-month delay will add up to about fifty million dollars in lost revenue overall — and thus, your Emotional Customer is equipped with fifty million votes in favor of your DV, and they outvote the Logical Customer who wants to block your sale.

This is why it is so important to understand and calculate TCOOL when you prepare to target your prospects and to think strategically when doing the DV exercise so you can pile up the consequences in all three time tenses (past, present, and future). In an economic democracy, every dollar's worth of pain and consequences equals one vote — and more votes will equip your Emotional Customer to override the Logical Customer who's blocking your sale.

Cost of Delay

The cost of delay is a tremendously important concept to accelerate the cadence of your sale. We want to know the approximate cost of delay experienced by the prospect enterprise for every month, week, or even day they delay adopting your DV.

The cost of delay is the little piece of magic that will accelerate the cadence of your sale. When you engage your prospects, you want the cost of delay on the table — and it must be their number, not yours. (You'll want to calculate it, too, but only to equip you ahead of the conversation. While talking to prospects, you'll never tell them the cost of delay! You'll only use their number, which they'll articulate in response to your excellent DV questions. We'll talk about those questions in Chapter 7.)

The cost of delay will be your greatest tool when the Logical Customer tries to drag their feet because they're isolated from the costs and consequences of delay. They may lie to you by saying: "We're really interested in what you have to offer — can we set aside some time next month for another demo?" (Remember, they're lying when they say they're "interested"!)

In response, you can invoke the cost of delay:

> *"We love doing demos and would be happy to, but I'm curious and have to ask — when you explained to the board that they'd have to live with another four weeks of this problem that's costing them about a million dollars a week so your team could see the demo again, what guidance did they give you?"*

Your question assumes they had the professional courtesy to inform the Emotional Customers of their decision to extend the problem. Of course, they probably haven't, and will likely reply with some vague answer that evades your question. That's okay; the important thing is to have asked the question so the cost of delay is on the table and it's clear that there are no free moves.

The DV Pyramid

We can visualize the effect of DV on our targeting and selling efforts using the following pyramid.

At the bottom of the pyramid are commodities — interchangeable items with no differentiation at all. These might include office supplies for corporations, bulk ingredients for food manufacturers, silica sand for computer chips, or iron ore for structural steel. It doesn't matter where these commodities are procured because each supplier is providing effectively the same thing. These commodities solve simple problems; the people worried about those problems are concerned with short time horizons (the next month) and are willing to change suppliers quickly. Sales are accomplished with quotes to the Purchasing department or RFPs and usually don't require salespeople. At this level, sales have no real margin, so high volumes are critical to success — that's why the pyramid is widest at the bottom.

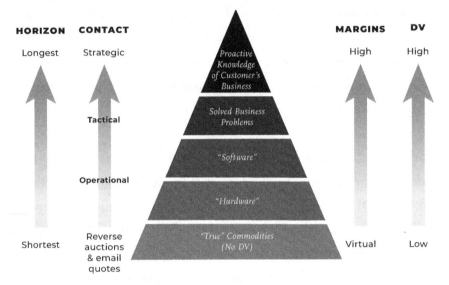

HORIZON	CONTACT		MARGINS	DV
Longest	Strategic	*Proactive Knowledge of Customer's Business*	High	High
	Tactical	*Solved Business Problems*		
	Operational	*"Software"*		
		"Hardware"		
Shortest	Reverse auctions & email quotes	*"True" Commodities (No DV)*	Virtual	Low

Toward the middle of the pyramid, we have solutions that solve operational problems. Software frequently occupies this middle area, but we might also see unique service providers or commodity suppliers who have some DV in their business model. (Examples might include project management software or commercial cleaning services.) The field here is crowded with competitors, but some differentiation is possible. The primary contact at the prospect organization will likely be someone who is focused on the near future, like project managers and engineers whose dashboards look ahead to the next quarter. Sales cycles may not be lightning fast, but they're still pretty short and transactional. Margins at this level are okay but not great because DV tends to be thin and focused on the present here.

If you have stronger DV, then you can move up the pyramid to target VPs and those who run business units; their dashboards look ahead up to two years. There are still a few competitors, but you can win more at higher margins. The competitive field might include some new technologies, but there are also basic service providers or commodity suppliers who have enough DV in their execution to compete at this level. Naturally, there are fewer competitors as you move up the spectrum because not many companies (or salespeople) fully understand what their DV is, let alone successfully wield it to win sales at those heights.

At the very top of the DV pyramid are high-margin, high-DV sales, where there are real and significant consequences to an enterprise for not buying what you sell. Those consequences may happen over a long time period, and as a result you'll be talking to executives whose strategic plans comprise a longer time horizon. If your strong DV solves strategic problems for high-ranking leaders, then this is the elevation you need to be selling at. There are very few competitors here.

The leaders at this high level in your prospect organization are not involved in day-to-day operations. They're concerned with future strategy; growth; mergers and acquisitions. Typically, company heads and board chairs have a three-to-five-year planning horizon, but those horizons may lengthen as you cross cultures and industries. Some industries with a heavy infrastructure investment, like energy, require a ten-year horizon. Non-Western companies might have an even longer horizon; Konosuke Matsushita, founder of Matsushita Electric (now Panasonic) in Japan famously had a 250-year strategic plan!

The more DV you bring to an enterprise, the more you can confidently target high-level leaders who understand that your DV can help them strategically. They'll grasp the strategic costs and consequences of keeping the problem you solve, and then they'll move decisively and quickly.

Use this pyramid as a reality check when you're using your DV to target the right prospects. If you think you're selling at high value, but you're talking to operations managers with ninety-day horizons, you're probably settling for a low-DV sale without realizing it, and your margins may be suffering.

Over the course of your complex sale, you will engage various players in the cast of characters at your prospect organization, and you will find yourself talking to people at various levels of this pyramid. That's fine — simply remember that what's important to a process engineer is not equally important to the executive in charge of launch strategy. Language is key here, and you must be ready to adjust your DV language as you move up and down the pyramid at your prospect organization. You will still be pointing to the same things in your conversations, but the time horizons and milestones will be different because how each person measures progress on their side is unique to their position.

If you're talking to an Emotional Customer in the C-suite, they'll care about the strategic opportunities they can't take advantage of over the next five years. If you're talking to a Process Engineer, they'll care about the rising expenses they're seeing on the horizon over the next six months, and you can talk about price vs. cost. If you're talking to the Third Assistant Junior IT Manager, they'll care about their team's experience today and will want a fourteenth demo just to make sure they like what you've got.

Simply remember that if you want to close your high-DV sale at high margins, you will ultimately need to engage the executives who care about the problems your DV can solve. You can interact with anyone along the pyramid as you cultivate the complete cast of characters, but do not fool yourself into thinking you'll get a high-DV sale closed in the lower tier. You need to climb higher to find targets who care about the problems your DV can solve.

We have a client — let's call them Streamlined Capital — whose technology solution helps reduce inefficiencies in large construction projects, with billions of dollars of savings available for very large enterprises. Their solution isn't cheap, but it's marvelously effective.

Streamlined Capital used to encounter a lot of resistance from Logical Customers in the middle tiers of this pyramid whose livelihoods depended on those inefficiencies. The Logical Customers knew instinctively that if our client's solution was installed, their job (managing the myriad delays) would disappear. Thus, the Logical Customer did everything they possibly could to slow down Streamlined Capital's sale, often acting really "interested" in order to sequester the sellers in endless conversations that ultimately went nowhere.

By working with us, Streamlined Capital learned to target the higher-ranking Emotional Customers instead — those who were frustrated by the inefficiencies but had no idea that improvement was even possible. Streamlined Capital began reaching out to the C-suite executives with strategic, prospect-focused DV language that resonated. Now they regularly close their seven-figure sale in two forty-five-minute conversations at that altitude. No endless cycles of demos, proof, quotes, questions, or resistance — just action.

Premature Pitch Symptom: *Can't Get Back to C-suite*

One thing is very important to remember about the Emotional Customer: They do not care about what you sell. They do not care about your features and benefits, how long your company has been in business, how you operate, your happy team culture, the old guy who founded the thing, or even what makes you amazing in the marketplace.

If you give a premature pitch to the Emotional Customer, talking about what you sell or how your solution is built, they will send you down to the Logical Customer, who specializes in talking to vendors like you about solutions like yours and commoditizing them.

This is because your Emotional Customer is not involved in day-to-day operations, and if you drop your language down to the tactical level (solution, system, offering, details, implementation, deadlines, etc.), they will quickly and correctly conclude that the conversation isn't worth their time. They'll be polite, but they will hand you off to the Logical Customer whose entire job it is to live in those details, and you'll have trouble getting back into conversations with the C-suite.

We have a client in cutting-edge technology — we'll call them Software, Inc. — who came to us because their salespeople were all highly skilled consultants who were having inexplicable trouble getting back to the C-suite for a second meeting. They'd done a great job consistently getting a first meeting at that elevation, and that first meeting had always gone "very well" — they'd established rapport, and the executive had seemed genuinely interested in what their solution could offer. But they just couldn't get back in for the second meeting they needed to move their sale forward.

It didn't take us long to figure out that these brilliant consultants, who had been trained throughout their careers to teach and tell, had been giving premature pitches, telling the executive all about the problems they fixed and how they fixed them. Their language was solution-oriented, all about "us" and how Software, Inc. solved these problems. The executive listened attentively but concluded that a solution this high-tech should be evaluated by their various technology teams (all Logical Customers) and that they wouldn't need to be involved in those conversations. As a result, Software, Inc.'s sellers were getting stuck at Wimp Junction with Logical Customers whose goal was to delay and commoditize the solution.

We helped Software, Inc. shift their language from being solution-centric and technical to being prospect-centric by walking them through the DV exercise and crafting strategic questions. We helped the sellers avoid teaching and telling on their calls, and focus on selling instead.

They asked questions that resonated with the Emotional Customer about the planned initiatives they hadn't yet been able to accomplish despite their best efforts (which Software, Inc.'s solution could ultimately help them achieve). This high-level, strategic, prospect-centric language allowed them to stay at the right elevation throughout their sale, getting it closed faster and avoiding the endless delays and pricing pressures that come with lower-level sales.

Talking about your solution — its features, benefits, specifications, or history — to the Emotional Customer will get you sent down to the Logical Customer. It is imperative to keep the focus of the conversation on THEM and their problems, not on you and your solution.

If your sales team has been struggling with getting a second appointment with the C-suite, the problem is likely a premature pitch. They went to solution. The executive heard it and said, "Ah! I see — we've got a guy for that," and sent them down to the Logical Customer where they never saw the light of day again.

Case Study: *Payers*

We have a client — let's call them Faster Claims — who sells a technology solution to health insurance providers. The innovative solution allows the insurance companies to spend less human labor time processing difficult claims, shrinking resolution time from approximately twelve weeks to less than one minute.

Before we started working together, Faster Claims' salespeople were targeting various Logical Customers — people whose titles seemed like a logical fit with their technology, like Head of Information Technology or Chief Innovation Officer. Their sales were getting stuck at Wimp Junction.

When we did the DV exercise together and answered the Cinnamon Question ("What's happening to whom because they're not our customer?"), Faster Claims discovered an entire category of Emotional Customers they had previously overlooked: Sales.

When an insurance provider takes twelve weeks to resolve one difficult claim for a member, that member gets frustrated. Frustrated members express their frustration to their employer's HR department. The employer's HR department determines which insurance plans will be available the next year. When enough member employees get frustrated by an insurance carrier, that employer will move their business to another carrier who can service their employee members better.

By shrinking resolution time from twelve weeks to seconds, Faster Claims wasn't just making operations smoother for the insurance company's back office — they were giving the insurance company a solid competitive advantage in the marketplace as they worked hard to land new employer accounts.

Who cares about that? The Chief Revenue Officer. THAT was the hallowed Emotional Customer for Faster Claims.

When they'd tried selling through Information Technology, Innovation, and Operations, they'd gotten a lot of interest but very little movement. All the players at their prospect organizations were wary of trying something new; they were reluctant to overhaul their worlds. They also had lots of innovative options to consider and all the time in the world to explore new ideas since the cost of delaying starting any one of them wasn't showing up on their dashboards.

But the Chief Revenue Officer was struggling daily with the monumental task of selling enough new accounts to replace all the companies leaving because it took the insurance company so long to resolve claims for their employees. That CRO needed the bleeding to stop. When Faster Claims began targeting CROs as their Emotional Customers, their traction in the marketplace improved enormously.

Case Study: *Aerospace*

We have a client — let's call them Aerospace, Inc. — who makes coatings for manufacturing parts in the aerospace engineering industry. They're small but growing, and they often compete against some entrenched giants in their sales.

Before we started working together, Aerospace, Inc.'s first point of contact at any prospect organization was always a Logical Customer: the Process Engineer (PE). The PE would always happily consider evaluating any supplier who could provide just two things: (1) a coating that fit the specifications and (2) the lowest price. Anything that happened outside the specs was irrelevant; the PE's time horizon was simply the length of the deal. They didn't care about life beyond the bid.

Aerospace, Inc. was losing deals to an entrenched giant who offered the lowest price in the marketplace by far but with a nasty twist: Over the life of the coating, the buyer would have to pay an annual fee to the giant based on how much coating they used in production. Remember the price vs. TCOOL (the Total Cost of Ownership Over the Life of a product)? This entrenched giant offered the lowest up-front price but taxed their customer on the deal for years afterward, driving up TCOOL astronomically.

The PE, being a Logical Customer, didn't care about TCOOL at all; that tax would be paid later, after the product hit the market and by other parts of the organization. He was isolated from the financial consequences of his decision. And he had incentive to keep the Entrenched Giant on as a vendor; he already knew the guy, he'd worked with him, it was comfortable. It would have been awkward for the PE to move business away from him. He had every incentive to minimize his own personal risk. Additionally, the PE was rewarded for his "price savings" every year; he would have had difficulty defending any switch to a "higher-priced" solution.

Aerospace, Inc. wanted to win a particularly large opportunity, so we helped them target their true Emotional Customer at the prospect organization: the Chief Financial Officer, who cared about their company's bottom line and whose time horizon was over the life of the product.

This CFO didn't care about manufacturing parts and didn't want to hear anything about materials or product specs. She did, however, care deeply about the ongoing financial health of the enterprise, which was unnecessarily suffering because of the tax on each item produced. This tax was eating into margins, causing results to come in lower than forecasted for years after the product launched.

Once Aerospace, Inc. targeted and engaged the CFO, the Emotional Customer, their DV was recognized: a clear, honest pricing structure that offered significantly lower TCOOL over many years. Aerospace, Inc. skillfully altered their prospect's decision-making process to value TCOOL over up-front price, and they won the deal.

The Logical Customer may make a natural first target for your prospecting efforts, but they will be difficult to sell on your Differentiating Value; they tend to be tire-kicking, bottom-feeding price suckers. The Emotional Customer won't care about what you sell (and will send you down to the Logical Customer if you start talking about your stuff), but will care deeply about alleviating the pain of their problem — the problem that your Differentiating Value can solve.

The Logical Customer Loves the Status Quo

Here is a very important thing to remember about Logical Customers: Even if they appear to be "in pain" while living with the consequences of the problem your solution can solve, they may not actually mind the problem at all. In fact, it may be job security for them. They tend to be heavily invested in the status quo.

We have one client — let's call them Hacker Geek — who sells custom software solutions. Before we began working together,

Hacker Geek often targeted Information Technology (IT) departments because those departments were living with the daily burden of using unstable, outdated, or just plain bad software. The IT folks were constantly patching temporary solutions together, and as a result, the software was running sub-optimally and requiring more and more frequent patches.

Hacker Geek, who hadn't yet finished the DV exercise above, defended their choice to target IT: "The IT department actually feels the pain! They're the ones living with the consequences of using old software! They're doing the workarounds; they're doing the patches. They know they need us. Our decision-maker in IT even tells us they need an overhaul soon, or the whole system will crash and they know it."

Yet ... the IT "decision-maker" had been sitting on a proposal for eight months (which is what prompted Hacker Geek's phone call to us).

Of course IT was aware of the workarounds and temporary patches — they were the architects behind them! Hacker Geek's solution was a threat to their world; they'd have to finally admit that their patches were inadequate. No one wants to admit their hard work isn't good enough. They were aware that their patchwork system would crash soon, and they needed some ideas to fix it, fast.

Thus, IT was very interested in learning the details of Hacker Geek's excellent solution because those details helped them improve their own work with the latest and greatest new information, and they could carry on with their DIY patching for another few years until heading to the lake for retirement. They had collected valuable, fresh information from Hacker Geek at Wimp Junction, applied the knowledge to patch the worst of the DIY gaps, and gone dark indefinitely.

Difference Between Interest and Pain

Do not mistake interest for pain. Logical Customers have interest; Emotional Customers have pain. Allow me to draw a quick case study on the difference between interest and pain.

When the anesthesiologist delivered my epidural to dull my labor pains before my first child arrived, I did not care what extra letters were behind the doctor's name, nor did I care what the liquid solution contained or how big the needle was. I had pain, and I needed it gone, STAT.

Any conversation regarding the above details would have simply added more fuel to my already-burning Irish-temper blaze. And if he'd pulled out a slide deck to explain any of the epidural's features and benefits, heaven help him; we'd have ended up on the six o'clock news.

My husband, however, was very interested in the details. His eyes widened when he saw the considerable size of the needle. He had questions about paralysis rates. He was deeply concerned about the doctor's aim as the latter drove the needle into my spinal column. He wanted to know how good (like, really how good) this anesthesiologist was.

My husband's questions could have delayed the entire exchange had he been allowed to run the decision. But my pain outweighed his interest, and the entire exchange was complete in under three minutes. *Interest doesn't get closure. Pain does.*

This is why there are so many pain-based selling systems out there. Human beings will move faster to avoid a pain than to achieve a pleasure (including satisfying one's interest) every single time. They will move to solve pain faster than they'll move to achieve "nice-to-haves" like features and benefits.

This is why we must remain unequivocally focused on the prospect's world and not on our features and benefits. What is this enterprise living with in the absence of your DV? What are they living with (past, present, and future) that your DV can solve? Isolation may keep the right people from recognizing the full tally, but your selling efforts will help overcome isolation so they can connect the dots and understand all the consequences they're really living with because they're not your customer — pain your solution can alleviate.

In an organization, that pain may look like missed strategic opportunities, looming future risks, or unsustainable TCOOL. It's critical to proactively identify the Emotional Customers who are living with that pain and target them.

Your Logical Customers will appear interested in your solution, but they're isolated from the costs of delaying its benefits. Your Emotional Customers, meanwhile, are the ones in pain, and they want the pain fixed, now. If you target the Emotional Customer with the right DV language, and you avoid the premature pitches that will get you sent down to the Logical Customer, you will probably find that the cadence of your sales accelerates considerably.

TACTICAL

We've talked about strategically determining who your real selling targets are. Now, let's talk about tactics to target them, with the goal of ultimately engaging them.

First, we'll distill your DV work into a single summary you can use in the marketplace to open up a conversation around your DV without landing at Wimp Junction. Then, we'll share with you a powerful targeting sequence to reach your Emotional Customers. We'll also share a few other ideas for targeting hard-to-reach prospects. Finally, we'll share a simple exercise to clarify the weekly targeting behaviors that will help you reach your goals.

A NOTE ABOUT PRE-CALL HOMEWORK

High-value sales require some pre-call homework. It is imperative that you research your target organizations before calling on the players in your cast of characters. You should know the most likely pains your prospect is experiencing because they're not your customer and how those pains are showing up in their life.

Validate your assumptions by looking up their recent financials if publicly available — where are they bleeding? How do they talk about themselves on their website? What do they say about their position in the marketplace? What mission strategies do they talk about that they're clearly having trouble achieving?

Sadly, many sellers skip this step because they're only planning to talk about themselves during the sales call. Since you won't be doing that, you need to be equipped with thorough intelligence on your prospect's world. Do your pre-call homework.

Distilling Your DV into a 30-Second Infomercial

Let's distill your Differentiating Value into a 30-Second Infomercial. This exercise sounds simple but is often quite difficult to execute because it requires cleansing our language of anything even remotely related to our amazing features and benefits. This DV statement must be entirely focused on our strategic target: the Emotional Customer.

In our work with thousands of companies, we've found that even once they understand their DV, most salespeople have a hard time putting the right words into play so that prospects understand and value it too. It's difficult to break the habit of talking about ourselves and the stuff we're selling.

Most persuasion messages tend to be some form of telling, informing, teaching, or presenting. According to marketing estimates, the average person gets three to four thousand messages a day telling them what to do with their time, their money, or their attention. If we package our DV into just another message telling our prospect what to do, they will tune us out.

Instead, we'll give a quick summary of our DV without talking about our "stuff" at all.

Imagine this scenario: You're standing in the lobby of your top prospect enterprise. You have not yet met your key Emotional Customer, but you recognize that person from your research. As the elevator door begins to close, that person steps in, then turns to you and says: "Good morning. What brings you in today?"

How do you package, into thirty seconds or less, a brief summary of your DV so this prospect doesn't tune you out? Remember, this is not a pitch!

An effective 30-Second Infomercial has these attributes:
+ Short
+ Focused on the consequences most likely to get a "That's me! I'd like to know more" reaction, rather than a "So what?" reaction
+ Starts with a one-sentence story to drop any defenses
+ Ends with a question that places an obligation on the other person to talk (the best Infomercials will use Open-Ended Questions)

Here is the template for preparing yours:

> *We work with [companies, people, teams, organizations, executives]*
> *who/that have already mastered [core competencies] and are:*
> *seeking ...*
> *determined ...*
> *in a position to ...*
> *certain they must ...*

Then: Insert a consequence from the Differentiating Value work you did.

At Slattery, our 30-Second Infomercial may begin like this:

> *"We work with executives who have already achieved high growth*
> *and are now seeking to enhance their margins beyond what they've*
> *already been able to accomplish so far."*

Notice that the focus is entirely on our clients and their results. We didn't say anything about how we achieve results because that would be too focused on us. *Results* are about the *prospect*; *how* we get those results is about us. This Emotional Customer doesn't care if we accomplish our results through weekly consulting or monthly training or proprietary frameworks or anything — they care only about the results: enhanced margins.

Also notice: We gave this person credit for work they've already done. This is so important! Too often, sellers inadvertently craft outreach messages with an accusatory tone: "Did you know you've been doing it wrong?" It's so easy to be accusatory because we're selling a solution — and when we're selling a solution, our starting point must necessarily be to assume our prospects have a problem worth solving; that's why we're selling a solution at all.

We must be incredibly careful to not call the prospect incompetent in their problem. The opening line of your engagement cannot sound like, "You have a problem! Did you know that? You probably don't!" That's simply calling them stupid. Instead, we must give credit to the prospect for their progress thus far and offer hope that perhaps things could be better beyond what they've already accomplished.

> *"We work with executives who have already achieved high growth and are seeking to enhance their margins beyond what they've already been able to accomplish so far."*

But we're not done! We must always end with a question if we want our statement to lead to a conversation at all. Otherwise, we'll simply keep talking, which carries high risk of our slipping into a premature pitch the prospect never requested. We must stay prospect-centric.

Shift the conversation to them by ending each statement with an Open-Ended Question:

- *"What is ... ?"*
- *"Where are you ... ?"*
- *"How would you ... ?"*
- *"How open would you be ... ?"*
- *"If you could ... ?"*
- *"Which is ... ?"*

Please note that these are Open-Ended Questions that prompt rich, full answers. If you revert to asking a closed-ended question instead (like "could we" or "would you be"), then you'll get a yes-or-no answer, and you'll end up talking again. The goal is for us to talk less and for the prospect to talk more. (We'll go into more detail about using Open-Ended Questions in your sales conversations in Chapter 6.)

A finished product of our 30-Second Infomercial might sound like this:

> *"We work with executives who have already achieved high growth and are seeking to enhance their margins beyond what they've already been able to accomplish so far. How open would you be to a brief conversation to see if the results we achieve might have interest for your enterprise?"*

Another version might sound like this:

> *"We have developed unique tools for companies seeking to significantly increase either the volume or the profitability of their sales. Which of those is currently the higher priority for your business: volume or profitability?"*

Craft a few different versions of this infomercial and find the version you're most comfortable using. Then say it out loud many times, until you're at ease and congruent. "Congruent" is a term we use in sales training circles — it means that you, the seller, believe what you're saying. If you're not congruent with yourself, your prospect's nervous system will pick up on tiny little triggers alerting them to the incongruence, and you'll lose their trust. Build congruence through repetition, like an actor rehearsing their lines. Practice this infomercial until muscle memory takes over and you can do it in your sleep.

Be very careful to triple-check your work and ensure that you do not talk about your solution or how you achieve results for your customers (because that's a premature pitch about you, not them).

A poor version of mine might have sounded like this:

> *"We work with executives who have already achieved high growth and are seeking to enhance their margins with our unique blend of sales training, coaching, and consulting. How open would you be to a brief conversation to see if the tools we've developed might have interest for your enterprise?"*

Notice that I went to *how* we'd accomplish the results: sales training, coaching, and consulting. That's a premature pitch; I shouldn't be presenting "how we'll solve your problem" when they haven't yet agreed they have a problem. We must have the prospect's consent and cooperation at each step before moving forward, or we risk irritating them. Remember, prospects hate receiving presentations they didn't request; don't jump into one at "Hello." I'll get better results when I replace "sales training, coaching, and consulting" with more prospect-oriented concepts like "revenue and profitability."

When we do this exercise with clients, it usually takes a few rounds of editing to trim all the salesy language out of it. Be ruthlessly prospect-focused here. There is always a strong temptation to pepper in just a little bit of pitching about how we solve problems.

There's also a strong temptation to craft one single silver-bullet infomercial that will magically resonate with every prospect, everywhere. Beware the silver-bullet temptation! Specificity is your friend here; if your language is generic, it won't resonate at all. In my example above, I could broaden the language in an attempt to craft a silver bullet: "We help companies lift sales." That may be broad enough to generally apply to salespeople, sales managers, sales VPs, and CROs, but it won't resonate with the executive who's strategically focused on achieving higher margins — and that's my Emotional Customer. (More importantly, there are thousands of sales-training companies promising that very same vague thing!)

If you have different types of Emotional Customers, then craft a different laser-focused Infomercial for each one. Don't try to encapsulate all your prospects and all their problems into a single statement, or you'll overwhelm with words. It's better to craft a few different versions focused on the right prospects than a single summary that will prove useless in the marketplace.

When you're done crafting your 30-Second Infomercial (or Infomercials), please check to make sure it has:

- Clarity of concept — are you brief and clear?
- Consequence to prospect — are you focused on the prospect?
- No pitch — don't even mention your "stuff"
- No specs — don't talk about "how" you do it
- An Open-Ended Question at the end

Approaching Leads in a Cold Market with a Voicemail-Email Pairing System

Here is a practical and effective pattern for approaching leads in a cold market and leveraging your Differentiating Value (DV) to get a conversation.

It's a Voicemail-Email Pairing System designed to pique your target's interest by tapping into their likeliest pains (which your DV can solve) without putting them off.

It's rather easy to carry out, and we have numerous clients who have found excellent success by following this method. Our clients research their targeted niche, line up several leads to target, and then leave a series of strategic voicemails for those leads, often on a Sunday afternoon during football game commercials. They follow up with an email a few days later.

As with any DV-oriented language, nuance matters here! There are small details that can either enhance or sabotage your efforts, and I will point them out as we go.

Here's how the Voicemail-Email Pairing System works:

- You'll send four pairs of messages; in each, you will first leave a voicemail, then send an email. Note the ideal time intervals between messages, and between pairs.
- Each pair of messages is laser-focused on one single point of DV. (No silver bullets!)
- Before you plan your messages, make sure you have clarified your top three points of DV (see Chapter 4 to review) and have developed prospect-centric language around the costs and consequences of each.

- Keep your voicemails as far under thirty seconds total as you possibly can. Your emails will be kept equally focused and succinct.
- No pitches! Do NOT talk about your "stuff." Don't even mention what you sell.
- Expect no results until the fourth pair of messages. If you see any results before that, you're just getting lucky.
- Make sure you have current (as in, recently verified by a human) direct dial and email info.

Here's the framework for the message pairs:

VM Message #1

This message is about the pain and consequences your Emotional Customer is most likely experiencing by not having your DV Point #1.

> "Hi, [target first name], [your name] XXX-XXX-XXXX. We may not need to speak in person. I work with executives at your level who are not completely satisfied with the options being presented to them [to fix this pain or close this gap].
>
> If you call and get my voicemail, please leave two times when we can speak in person. XXX-XXX-XXXX."

Notice a few key points:

- Recite your phone number immediately so if they have to play the voicemail again to recapture it, they don't have to listen to the whole message again.

- Use a negative opening comment. Always. I'll explain why in the next chapter.
- No pitching! You're only mentioning a pain point. That's it.
- Unless you're selling for a major brand, don't bother mentioning your company name. It will only prompt your prospect to wonder, "Who?" and conclude that they don't know you and therefore don't need to call you back.

- Notice what we don't say:
  - We don't say anything about what we do or how we do it.
  - We don't say anything about our awesome features, benefits, savings, rainbows, kitties, or unicorns.
  - We don't say anything about how good life could be with us.
  - We don't say anything about how they're doing it wrong without us.
  - We don't even bother mentioning our last name (they don't care about it, it makes it obvious we're a stranger, and it costs precious seconds to say).

EM Message #1

This email follows up the first voicemail a day or so later, simply capturing it in written form.

> *Subject: [Insert relevant consequences of not having DV Point #1]*
>
> *"[Target first name]: Confirming my voice message of yesterday regarding possible [insert pain/consequences].*

If you're open to a brief conceptual conversation to see if there is value for you in what we've learned with XXX similar organizations, please reply with two times when we can explore it for a few minutes. Thanks."

Notice a few key points:

* There's nothing new here; the email simply summarizes the voicemail in written form. Resist the temptation to add more DV points; you'll risk cluttering your message.
* It's okay to have an email signature with your full name, company logo, link, etc. They may look you up and learn more about you and your company. This can build credibility. (That same information can sabotage a voicemail, though, causing the prospect to check out or conclude they don't know you.)
* Always invite them to a "brief" conversation. The word "brief" is important. You're reassuring them it won't last forever.

VM Message #2

This message is about the pain and consequences of not having your DV Point #2. Leave this voice message approximately four days after your email. Remember, only one DV Point at a time — no silver bullets!

"Hi, [target first name], [your name] XXX-XXX-XXXX. I know you get many messages and may not recall my previous message about [briefest possible review of DV Pain #1 consequences]."

Since I've not heard from you, that may mean you'd prefer to know [introduce consequences associated with DV Pain #2].

If you call and get my voicemail, please leave two times when we can speak in person. XXX-XXX-XXXX."

EM Message #2

This email follows up the second voicemail a day or so later, simply capturing it in written form.

Subject: [Insert relevant consequences of not having DV Point #2]

[Target first name]: Confirming my voice message of yesterday regarding possible [insert pain/consequences].

If you're open to a brief conceptual conversation to see if there is value for you in what we've learned with over XXX similar organizations, please reply with two times when we can explore it for a few minutes. Thanks.

VM Message #3

This message is about the pain and consequences of not having your DV Point #3. Leave this voice message approximately four days after your last email.

"Hi, [target first name], [your name] XXX-XXX-XXXX. I know you get many messages and may not recall my previous message about [briefest possible review of DV Pain #2 consequences].

Since I've not heard from you, that may mean you'd prefer to know [introduce consequences associated with DV Pain #3].

If you call and get my voicemail, please leave two times when we can speak in person. XXX-XXX-XXXX."

EM Message #3

This email follows up the third voicemail a day or so later, simply capturing it in written form.

Subject: [Insert relevant consequences of not having DV Point #3]

[Target first name]: Confirming my voice message of yesterday regarding possible [insert pain/consequences].

If you're open to a brief conceptual conversation to see if there is value for you in what we've learned with over XXX similar organizations, please reply with two times when we can explore it for a few minutes. Thanks.

In the fourth pair, you will gently (gently!) mention going away. This is generally what will spur them to action.

VM Message #4

This is the briefest possible review of the pain and consequences of not having your DV Point #3 — and a suggestion that you'll leave them alone. Leave this voice message approximately four days after your last email.

Use caution here — it's very easy to miss the nuance and sound like a jerk.

"Hi, [target first name], [your name] XXX-XXX-XXXX. I know you get many messages and may not recall my previous message about [briefest possible review of DV Pain #3 consequences].

Since I have not heard from you, that may mean I'm too early in bringing these options, and you'd like for me to go away. If that is not what you want me to do, and you call and get my voicemail, please leave two times when we can speak in person. XXX-XXX-XXXX."

EM Message #4

This email follows up the fourth voicemail a day or so later, simply capturing it in written form.

Subject: [Insert briefest possible review of the pain and consequences of not having DV Point #3]

"[Target first name]: Confirming my voice message of yesterday regarding possible [insert pain/consequences].

Since I've not heard from you, it may mean I am too early in bringing these options to you, and I should move on.

When you are open to a brief conceptual conversation to see if there is value for you in what we've learned with over XXX similar organizations, please reply with two times when we can explore it for a few minutes. Thanks."

The fourth message tends to be the magic moment — your offer to move on will often spur them to action. Human nature tends to want what it can't have. You'll most likely make contact here.

This "moving on" isn't a new tactic; it's extremely common in the sales marketplace, and has been for years. I get emails from sellers attempting this magic every week, and most of them are poorly done. They sound abrasive, impatient, or huffy, especially on the heels of poorly-planned outreach messages. I got a curt "moving on" message yesterday from a seller who had sent me just two weak emails (no voicemails, nothing else) completely focused on them and their solution. I never learned what they could do for me. As you can imagine, their petulance didn't exactly move the needle for me to take action.

Thus, this last message pair — and the complete Voicemail-Email Pairing Sequence — takes some thought. You want four complete pairs of messages. Each email must be preceded by a voicemail, so you make contact by voice first — this will make you sound human. Each pair must be ruthlessly prospect-centric and focused on only one point of DV — no more. And your offer to leave them alone in the fourth pair is an offer of courtesy, not impatience. Tread carefully.

If you still get no response after the fourth message pair, then this particular lead goes back into your company's nurture process for ten more spaced, automated marketing touches.

Since we've done this exercise with innumerable salespeople, I must reiterate a few critical points of nuance:
1. When crafting your Voicemail-Email Pairing System, the silver-bullet temptation remains strong! Do not put everything you solve into a single message, or you'll confuse your prospects. Make sure every message is laser-focused on one (and *only* one)

point of DV. Go back and check your work. Did you use the words "and" or "or"? If so, you may be trying to fit two pains into one message; go back and trim it down to one.

2. Do not underestimate how tempted you will be to talk about WHAT you do and HOW you do it. Go back and edit your sequence, ruthlessly removing any mention of WHAT you do or HOW you do it. That's about you. These messages must be prospect-centric, or you'll risk irritating your prospect with premature pitches they didn't request.

3. Always leave a voicemail first; the human connection you create with your voice is what gives your later email context.

4. Remember that your mental starting point is the assumption that your prospect has a problem you can solve. Therefore, you're at risk of sounding arrogant or abrasive. Take extra care to make sure you're not announcing that they have a problem or indicating that they've been "doing it wrong." Give them credit for what they've done so far. Don't inadvertently call them incompetent.

5. Don't be a jerk about the last pair of messages. As I write this, I'm still rolling my eyes at an attempted "moving on" email I just received this morning headlined, "We're breaking up." Don't be coy, cute, or clever. Be courteous — you're offering to give them some space by going away. Remember, we don't get anywhere without our prospect's consent and cooperation; we're the ones infringing on their inboxes, so let's be conscientious about it.

Other Outreach Tactics for Success

Targeting your ideal prospects is becoming increasingly difficult. In our experience at Slattery over the last four decades, the number of marketing touches to bring a prospect from "Who are you?" to "Let's meet" is increasing. We used to tell clients to count on about ten to twelve touches, but now it's about sixteen to twenty. Prospects are harder than ever to reach, and they're getting better at tuning out noise like advertisements, outreach messages, and voicemails. Don't give up early; when you have DV, and your messages reflect an understanding of your prospect's world, all your outreach efforts will help you get traction in the marketplace and fill your pipeline.

This does mean, however, that your prospecting efforts must be laser-focused on the right prospects: the Emotional Customers. You don't have spare time or resources to spend targeting Logical Customers who will gladly engage you for some Unpaid Consulting.

It also means that your prospecting efforts must be laser-focused on all the consequences this prospect is likely living with in the absence of your DV. If you talk about your solution, you'll risk sounding exactly like all the other salespeople who are pitching to the same prospect using the same language, and you'll only commoditize yourself and lengthen your sales cycle by being part of the noise.

It also means that you need to plan extra touches. We offer eight with the voicemail-email sequence above; you'll want at least a dozen other touches ready to leverage as you reach out to your possible Emotional Customers. But these touches must still be prospect-centric (or you risk sounding like other sellers) and focused on what they're living with in the absence of your DV.

We recommend collecting a handful of useful white papers or timely articles that you can send to your prospects. This is why it's so helpful to proactively identify your Emotional Customers! If you realize that your Emotional Customers are CFOs, then you can curate a handful of articles that would bring CFOs value. (They can be relevant white papers produced by your enterprise, but we strongly recommend finding well-respected outside sources like *Wall Street Journal* articles, Harvard Business Review case studies, industry papers, etc. This keeps the focus away from you and on your prospect.)

On that point, when you send a white paper or article, make sure it is actually useful to them. It should not be about you and your solution; rather, it should be something very relevant to their world (and what they're living with in the absence of your DV, but of course you'll never mention that). If they're a manufacturing CEO, then you might send them an industry-specific interview on strategies that work when supply chains are disrupted. Simply send it with a short note: "Saw this and thought of you."

The point here is to earn the right to have a conversation. Bring value first. Make deposits into the relationship before you ask for something like a meeting; you haven't earned the right to their time yet.

Incidentally, you will also distinguish yourself from your competitors in the marketplace who are talking about themselves and sounding salesy. You'll also establish your consultant-level credibility and expertise, since your laser-focused outreaches will indicate the depth of your knowledge about your prospect's world.

Make deposits. Bring value. Be patient. Stay focused on them. Be human.

Targeting Cadence: *Non-Negotiable Weekly Behaviors*

As a salesperson, you are responsible for turning a lead into a Customer by properly targeting and engaging them through your sales process. You need to close a certain number of opportunities each quarter or year, and every day you're working toward those goals.

Sales results are simply the sum of sales behaviors over time. At Slattery, we do a simple exercise with our clients to map out the behaviors that will help achieve those ambitious goals.

We begin the exercise by drawing five boxes, as below. This exercise clarifies exactly what it takes to close one single opportunity — because once we know what it takes to close one, we know what it takes to close all the sales that make up our goal.

Every market is different, and every company is different, but there is still a path all sales activities follow in order to close a deal. The path begins in the Targeting stage when you make a certain number of Approaches in order to land some Initial Discussions. From these discussions will emerge a few Qualified Prospects to whom you'll present an offer to do business. From those presentations, you'll close one opportunity.

The flow looks like this, from left to right:

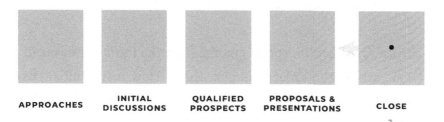

| APPROACHES | INITIAL DISCUSSIONS | QUALIFIED PROSPECTS | PROPOSALS & PRESENTATIONS | CLOSE |

1

The steps are the same in every sale, but the numbers in the boxes will vary. With your knowledge of your own company, industry, and sales cycle, begin at the right side by writing "1" in the box on the far right to indicate one closed sale.

Then, work backward from right to left by answering these questions:

1. In order to close one opportunity, how many proposals or presentations to do business must you put on the table, based on your current closing rate?

Let's say you'll need three proposals or presentations to close one deal. (Yes, we can enhance our closing rates later, but let's start with current reality now.)

2. Before each proposal or presentation, you must first engage a certain number of Qualified Prospects, not all of whom will make it to the presentation stage because they'll drop off through more rigorous qualification. How many Qualified Prospects will net those presentation opportunities you listed in #1?

Let's say you'll need eight engagements with Qualified Prospects to net three proposals or presentations.

3. Those Qualified Prospects emerge from the Initial Discussions you carry out in order to qualify them. How many Initial Discussions do you typically have to conduct in order to find the Qualified Prospects you listed above?

Let's say you need twenty Initial Discussions, from which emerge your eight Qualified Prospects.

4. Those valuable Initial Discussions happen only after you've made an even higher number of early Approaches to leads. How many Approaches did you have to make in order to have those twenty Initial Discussions?

Let's say you need to make sixty Approaches in order to get twenty good Initial Discussions.

In our example, our numbers look like this:

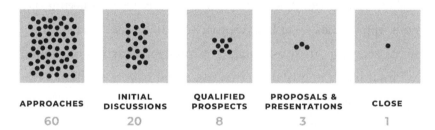

APPROACHES	INITIAL DISCUSSIONS	QUALIFIED PROSPECTS	PROPOSALS & PRESENTATIONS	CLOSE
60	20	8	3	1

This means that we must make sixty good Approaches in order to close one sale. Think of this flow as one "batch" of activity.

Now, we can extrapolate the number of Approaches that are necessary to close the total number of sales we need to make our goal for the year.

It's wise to add extra cushion by aiming for more than your goal because you will always encounter obstacles or circumstances outside your control (Murphy's Law), and you don't want to be overly reliant on any one opportunity. If your goal is four sales in a year, plan for six to be safe and boost your Approach numbers accordingly.

As you master additional selling skills, you will find that your math will improve and your sales cycle will shorten. But for now, start with your current "hit" numbers. That is the basis for your weekly non-negotiable activity levels.

If our goal is to close four sales in a year, and we want the cadence to remain steady enough to execute well, then we must finish the first batch of activity during Quarter 1 (at the latest). This means we must make sixty good Approaches that will result in one sale. It's wise to get them out of the way as soon as possible. (If you decide to space it out, then you must make five Approaches each week to get to sixty Approaches over the thirteen weeks in the quarter.)

Then, in Quarter 2, we work on our second batch, making sixty more Approaches — or five Approaches each week. Quarter 3 will see us starting our third batch, and probably starting our fourth and final batch to give ourselves some end-of-year cushion. (Plan on being done by mid-November at the latest to stay ahead of the holiday season.)

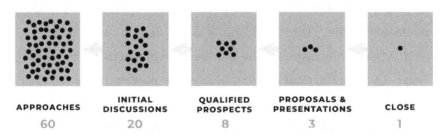

APPROACHES	INITIAL DISCUSSIONS	QUALIFIED PROSPECTS	PROPOSALS & PRESENTATIONS	CLOSE
60	20	8	3	1

Do not wait until Quarter 4 to begin your Approaches. Complex sales take time. If your sales cycle is twelve months long, then today is exactly one year from now already. What do you need closed by that date? Start doing the Approaches that are necessary now.

At Slattery, we call these Approaches the Non-Negotiable Weekly

Behaviors, or NNWB. Once you write down the numbers unique to your sales cycle, and you calculate how many batches you need to make your goal for the year, then you know what your NNWBs are each week.

Be ruthless in executing these NNWBs!

CHAPTER SIX

Engage – Part 1

The Prospect's Buying System		Your System
STEP 1		**STAGE 1**
The prospect lies to the salesperson.		*Differentiate*
STEP 2		**STAGE 2**
The prospect gets the salesperson to provide valuable information and a quote.		*Target*
		STAGE 3
STEP 3		*Engage*
The prospect lies about what's going to happen next.		**STAGE 4**
		Commit
STEP 4		**STAGE 5**
The prospect doesn't answer or return the salesperson's calls.		*Secure*

So you found your Emotional Customer — what do you talk about?

STRATEGIC

The ultimate outcome of our selling efforts is to successfully convince our prospect enterprise to go through the pain of change and adopt what we're selling. Selling is never easy, but in a complex sale, this simple goal is further complicated by the fact that we must engage multiple players in the cast of characters, all of whom have different priorities, and continue our forward cadence with their cooperation.

This means you'll probably have many sales calls with various people in your prospect organization over the course of each opportunity you pursue. You don't have endless time and resources to spend on infinite conversations as you engage your prospects, so it's critically important to gain clarity around the purpose of your sales calls so you can protect your limited resources and ultimately your margins.

Purpose of Sales Calls

We often ask our new clients when we start working together, "What is the purpose of your sales calls?" We get a variety of answers:

- "To educate our prospects."
- "To show what we offer."
- "To get to know each other."

There may not be anything wrong with those things, but they aren't precisely selling. They do not move your opportunity forward at an acceptable cadence to be worth the time and investment in a complex sale.

At Slattery, we consider a sales call to have just one purpose: to extend the conversation and collect information to determine if this is an opportunity worth pursuing.

Anything that doesn't both extend the conversation and help us determine if this is an opportunity worth pursuing isn't a sales call.

Control the Call

Sales calls require the investment of your most valuable selling resource: time. You don't have time to wander with interested prospects through endless conversations and demos. It's critical to control the conversation in order to move your opportunity forward at an acceptable cadence.

When you control the conversation, you collect the information you need to determine if this is an opportunity you can win — and you do it while maintaining your prospect's cooperation and goodwill.

But please note: While we control the conversation, we do NOT control the other person! This is an important distinction. We remain in control of the conversation by staying humble, focusing on the other human, and asking questions. Manipulative selling tactics have no place here.

In this chapter, I'll share with you ten Communication Keys we use at Slattery to help sellers control their sales calls so they can keep their prospect's goodwill and extend the conversation long enough to determine if this is an opportunity worth pursuing. These Communication Keys will help you run conversations around your value without alienating your prospect.

Nuance is important here. Over the decades in which we've been sharing these methods with clients, we've seen countless salespeople gloss over them, miss the nuance, and then go on to spectacularly botch their sales conversations.

The Foundation of Call Control

In 1967, Thomas Anthony Harris published a self-help book called *I'm OK–You're OK*. It was a practical approach to solving problems of social interactions and was based on transactional analysis. It introduced the ideas of "OK" and "Not OK," which have been enormously helpful for us in illustrating the importance of humility in sales conversations.

Imagine this scenario: Every conversation you have with another human being is happening in a sparsely furnished room in your mind. This room has just two chairs; one chair is for you, and the other chair is for the person you're talking to. (There's a similar setup of two chairs in their mind too.)

One of those chairs is called the "OK" chair, and the person who's sitting in it feels comfortable, confident, relaxed — they're okay.

The other chair is the "Not OK" chair, and the person who's sitting in it does not feel okay; they feel uncomfortable, and maybe even belittled or threatened.

Only one person at a time can occupy each chair, and everyone wants to be in the OK chair. To get in it, they must put the other person into the Not OK chair. They do this with words or actions that imply correcting, judging, telling the other person what to do, or even putting them down. "I'm right, you're wrong" is classic OK / Not OK positioning.

The confidence most salespeople are programmed with is the one thing most likely to sabotage their conversations. The very presence of the salesperson says, "We have a better way of doing things, and we know more than you do!" That's a one-way ticket to putting the prospect in the Not OK chair — and the prospect will therefore not cooperate.

One of the first questions we get when we describe this scenario is: Why can't both chairs be OK chairs? The answer is that they can, and in *your* head, they should be — but very few people are emotionally healthy enough to sit in the OK chair themselves and allow everyone else to be in one too. (Try giving someone constructive criticism and see how fast they fight you to get back in the OK chair.)

One quick glance at the world around us confirms that most people are Not OK most of the time: Their marriage is on the rocks, their kids are fighting, their work stinks, their boss is critical, and the wider world is falling apart. Very few people are comfortably settled into the OK chair in their own head, and they will try hard to claim it as soon as they can by knocking the other person into the Not OK chair instead.

So it doesn't matter if you have two OK chairs in your head; what matters is what your prospect expects in their head. If you appear to take the OK chair in their head, they will fight you for it so they're not stuck with the Not OK chair. This will manifest when they relish rejecting you, when they tell you they're doing fine without you, and when they push back on your declarations of awesomeness. They will not be comfortable until they've plopped you into the Not OK chair in their mind.

Therefore, in all your interactions, you need to consciously, graciously, intentionally take the Not OK chair first. And you'll do this with small, gentle, humble indicators: You don't need the OK chair. They can take it. They can be comfortable around you.

This doesn't mean you become a doormat! In fact, the rest of this chapter is devoted to methods to help you control the conversation so you can steer it where you need it to go; you're at the mercy of no one. This entire book is devoted to methods to help you control the entire sale so you don't end up on the prospect's side of the tracks at Wimp Junction. You remain in control to sell at high value.

To achieve this, however, we must proactively ensure the prospect's comfort during the conversation. This is ridiculously difficult for most humans, who are already Not OK and feel a need to prove themselves as the best and the brightest in the room by "winning" every conversation. And it's a thousand times harder for great sellers, the very humans who have been taught for decades to exude confidence when they enter the marketplace.

But selling from the Not OK chair will win you the engagement of more prospects, faster. They'll cooperate with you willingly. You can always remain confident, relaxed, and permanently settled into the OK chair in your own mind. Just don't fight your prospect for the OK chair in THEIR mind. In a word, be humble.

Remember, your prospect thinks they were doing just fine before you came along. The last thing they want is for you to waltz in and start telling them they were doing it wrong without you. That's putting them in the Not OK chair before you've even started selling.

People expect correction, lectures, confrontation, and admonition, especially from hyper-informed salespeople. Their defenses are up. They're not listening to your facts; they're listening for shots. But if you use Not OK language, you indicate that you're unarmed. They can relax. You're not there for conflict.

If you fill the Not OK chair in the conversation, then they'll be free to occupy the OK chair — and you'll find that they'll be much more willing to engage with you.

We worked with one client in manufacturing — we'll call them Precision, Inc. — whose salesperson did great DV work with us and then crafted a Voicemail-Email Pairing System to target his Emotional Customers. When the Voicemail-Email sequence failed to gain any traction for him in the marketplace, he concluded that something must be wrong with the sequence we taught him.

We asked for the chance to review his script. When we saw it, we found that even though he'd done a great job leveraging his DV and crafting messages that were brief and succinct, he was inadvertently taking a shot at his prospect in each message. He didn't mean to do this, but he was in the habit of sounding confident, and each message unfortunately came across with strong undertones of, "You've been doing it wrong, but luckily I'm here to help you, and I know more than you do!"

The OK / Not OK dynamic is real. Humans are remarkably sensitive creatures. I know the world has been telling you for decades to find yourself, express yourself, and not worry about how other people see you (and if they don't like you, too bad for them!). But great sellers don't have the luxury of endless self-expression in the marketplace. Great sellers must value the other human's perspective in every conversation and adjust their self-expression to accommodate the other human so they can earn the right to the next conversation. This is what makes great selling such a beautiful, rare, and important skill.

At Slattery, this concept of humility is central to everything we do. There isn't a selling system in the world that will work when the human executing it is abrupt, abrasive, or grabbing the OK chair in every conversation — whether they intend to or not.

Back in the 1980s, Terry worked with a manufacturing company — let's call them Supply, Inc. — that was expanding from California into the Midwest. Supply, Inc. had hired an excellent sales representative with a proven track record and great skills. This sales rep was able to get appointments with company owners but was having trouble getting any traction in the marketplace. Supply, Inc. wanted our help to diagnose what was going wrong in his new territory.

This sales rep flew from California to Minneapolis, where Terry met him at the airport. Terry watched passengers file into the baggage claim area and immediately picked out this sales rep from the crowd, because, in Terry's words, "He looked like a human condominium." He was a competitive body builder who stood 6 feet 4 inches tall with a flawless California tan and curly, blond, permed hair, and he was wearing an expensive custom-made shirt that was about three sizes too small (by Midwestern standards).

Terry immediately knew why this guy wasn't getting any traction in the marketplace: He was calling on sixty-year-old owners of small manufacturing companies across the Midwest who all had potbellies. The moment this sales rep walked into their office, they were instantly Not OK. There was nothing he could say about what he was selling or the problems he solved that would make them want to engage with him.

Terry said, "Before we go on our first sales call, we have a stop to make." They found a tailor who could provide a sport coat quickly. Terry instructed the sales rep to don it before walking into every sales call. This sport coat helped cover the chiseled muscles but didn't solve the height problem. The height problem arose when this sales rep gained entrance to a company owner's office — he walked in at full height while the owner was seated behind his desk. The disparity, which would have been significant even if they'd both been standing, was massive, with the sales rep inadvertently towering over the prospect.

So Terry instructed him to immediately ask the company owner permission to take a seat in his office. He said, "I don't care if you find a chair or if you have to go to a couch or anything else — do whatever you must to get yourself closer in altitude to that guy's height as soon as humanly possible."

Asking permission is a powerful tool, and it worked for this sales rep. After saying "Hello," he immediately got permission to sit down every time. As soon as he sat down, the dynamic in the room was significantly more equal. The prospect was more comfortable and feeling more OK.

Then, this sales rep asked permission to ask a few questions to see if what Supply, Inc. offered might have value for this owner. With the OK / Not OK dynamic balanced, the conversation commenced, and our rep could move forward with his skillful selling as usual.

The ultimate purpose of your sales calls is to extend the conversation with your prospect in order to determine if this is an opportunity worth pursuing. Without the humility we're describing here, you will not earn the extended conversation you need to qualify your opportunity.

The Last Mile of selling is the mile of human-to-human conversations. No matter how awesome your solution may be, in the Last Mile you are completely dependent on the cooperation of the other human being for the conversation to continue. If you lead with humility and let them take the OK chair in every conversation, you'll find you can maintain their goodwill and avoid unnecessary delays and stalls that might otherwise be triggered by inadvertent abrasiveness or arrogance.

Next, we'll dig into ten Communication Keys we teach our clients to help them control a sales call so they can extend the conversation and determine if this is an opportunity worth pursuing.

TACTICAL

Call Control Methods: *Ten Communication Keys*

Many sales methods and sales processes are designed with the seller in mind. They're structured to help the seller get in front of prospects faster, persuade more effectively, or track deals more easily. These are all good things, but without an even heavier focus on the prospect, they risk pushing the seller into salesy behaviors that trip the prospect's anti-salesperson defenses (remember, no one wants to be sold to!).

At its heart, the Slattery philosophy is laser-focused on the prospect and on keeping them in the OK chair — not because we're any less ruthlessly focused on winning the business, but because such humility is utterly critical to winning the business, and even the next conversation.

The Ten Communication Keys we share with you here are the ways we've learned to keep the prospect engaged and moving forward at an acceptable cadence.

COMMUNICATION KEY 1
Sell, Don't Tell

Remember No-Fail Selling Rule #2: Sell, don't tell. Telling is not selling. Telling — i.e., making declarative statements — plops your prospect into the Not OK chair in their mind because you're telling them that *you know more than they do.* They will not be comfortable in the conversation until they've knocked you out of the OK chair and taken it back — either by refuting whatever you told them or by dismissing you.

This dynamic of telling and debating makes selling much more difficult and time-consuming than it needs to be. To fix the problem, sellers often try to become better at telling: They'll be more engaging, more persuasive, more rapport-building, more credible, more authoritative. But every declarative statement, no matter how well-delivered, still risks putting your prospect into the Not OK chair from which they won't cooperate with you.

Telling also relinquishes control of the conversation to the other person. When you make declarative statements, your prospect doesn't have to engage; they can simply listen while you spend precious time and breath giving them more and more information, likely ending up at Step 2 of Wimp Junction with a premature pitch.

Telling isn't selling. Selling is getting the other person to talk so you can collect the information you need to qualify the opportunity. When the prospect talks, they articulate their pains. When they articulate their pains, they increasingly feel the weight of those pains on the scale in their mind, and the scale tilts in our favor. And we find out if the problem we think we've identified is present AND worth the pain of solving. Otherwise, we're there too early.

To learn about our prospect's problems and pains, we must ask questions. To help them articulate the costs and consequences they're experiencing in the status quo, we must ask questions. To qualify the opportunity, we must ask questions. To keep them in the OK chair and earn their cooperation, we must ask questions. To avoid Wimp Junction, we must ask questions.

The importance of asking questions isn't exactly a new concept; there are numerous books written about asking questions on sales calls. But we've found over the last four decades with more than 2,400 companies that even when sellers are in the habit of asking great questions, they're often not yet in the habit of not *telling*.

Avoid telling your prospect things. Let them answer your skillfully-asked questions, and collect the information you need to move forward efficiently.

COMMUNICATION KEY 2
Nurture, Don't Interrogate

Asking questions puts you in control of the conversation. Your prospect has been conditioned from childhood that when someone asks you a question, it's polite to answer. They won't let silence linger. Questions, when asked skillfully, will prompt your prospect to talk to you.

Unfortunately, when a seller asks questions, the conversation dynamic can quickly turn into interrogation mode — especially if they're asking questions from the OK chair, where they know more than their prosect. Prospects feel the heat of interrogation and disengage.

Ask questions, but don't interrogate your prospect. This requires nuance. You're not there to reenact a crime-show drama with your prospect as lead suspect. You're there to learn whether or not you have a Qualified Selling Opportunity, and you'll only move forward if you have your prospect's cooperation.

To ensure their cooperation, you must be nurturing with your questions. You must recognize that you are one human being dealing with another human being — one who can pick up on veiled insults, will get defensive if interrogated, and thinks they were doing fine before you came along.

The first way to nurture is to get permission to ask questions at the outset: "May I ask you a few questions?" It's simple, but it's critical to get buy-in from your prospect. Don't skip it.

Then, when you're in the conversation and you're asking your questions, there's one simple way to keep it feeling more friendly than confrontational: *Recognize* each answer before you respond with another question.

All you need is a small verbal recognition like, "That sounds reasonable," or, "That makes sense." Even a simple "Mm-hmm" lets your prospect know that you heard their answer. This says you're listening. (They don't even get this kind of nurturing at home.) This says you're hearing their answers, which encourages them to continue conversing. When you recognize their answer before responding, you keep the tone of the conversation humane and thoughtful.

Beware the temptation to drop the recognition as tension escalates. When prospects push back, salespeople often drop the recognition piece and jump straight to the next question they were planning to ask. Unfortunately, this accelerates the conversation and unnecessarily ratchets up the tension even further. It begins to sound like an awkward crime-show interrogation, and the prospect disengages.

For example, the prospect may declare, "We really like our current provider." The rookie seller jumps straight to their next question without even recognizing the prospect's statement: "What if they're not doing a great job mitigating all your risks?" It sounds awkward, and the prospect can sense the seller's discomfort.

To keep your prospect's engagement, simply recognize their answers before asking your next question. They tell you, "We really like our current provider." You recognize and respond: "Well, you're a longstanding customer, and I'm sure they appreciate your business. When they came by for their last quarterly site visit" — which you know they didn't do — "to assess your current risk profile, what were their recommendations?"

RECOGNIZE **RESPOND**

Take care of the other person **+** *Then, take care of business*

Tip: When you're doing a Recognize + Respond, don't use "I understand" as a Recognize tool. Prospects hate it. It sounds fake. You don't understand; you haven't walked in their shoes, and you haven't experienced the pain they're feeling in their position. Don't say, "I understand."

COMMUNICATION KEY 3
Open-Ended Questions

When you're asking questions, use Open-Ended Questions that start with Who, What, When, Where, and How. These questions prompt full, rich answers. They will compel your prospect to give you the information you need.

If you ask closed-ended questions like "Did you ...", "Are you ...", "Could we ...", or "Is it ...", you'll only prompt your prospect to answer with a yes or a no. And they'll stop there — their conversational obligation is fulfilled, and the next move is yours. They'll wait for you to talk next, and talk you will.

So many salespeople ask easy closed-ended questions, get a yes-or-no answer, and then talk for the rest of the sales call, which inevitably produces a premature pitch about the solution until the prospect can finally shut them up with a false promise to "think it over" (Step 3 at Wimp Junction!).

Beware the overwhelming temptation to switch Open-Ended Questions to closed-ended questions. We see even highly skilled sellers do this all the time. They intend to ask an Open-Ended Question like, "How open would you be to a brief discussion ... ?" but inadvertently switch it to, "Could we have a brief discussion ... ?" It takes heightened awareness to keep your questions open.

If you ask closed-ended questions, you'll lose control of the conversation and lose the chance to qualify this sales opportunity. Keep your questions open-ended. You're here to gain information.

COMMUNICATION KEY 4
Don't Ask Why

On the heels of #3, here's one Open-Ended Question you never want to ask: "Why?"

The word *why*, more than any other word in the English language, puts people into the Not OK chair. Avoid it at all costs.

When you ask "Why?" the other person in the conversation can only answer with some kind of self-defense: "Because I ..." Don't put your prospect in that chair. Remember, most people are Not OK to start with. Asking your prospect "Why?" can destroy the trust and rapport you've worked hard to establish.

We once worked with a client — we'll call them Premium Software — who hired us to work with a salesperson who was having trouble getting traction in the marketplace. This person was a subject-matter expert who knew everything there was to know about the solution and the problem it solved. To Premium Software, they seemed like a natural fit to sell the solution.

Unfortunately, this subject-matter expert wasn't strong at selling, and after riding with them for one round of sales calls, we quickly perceived the risk to Premium Software of having them in the field.

This subject-matter expert was a kind and wonderful human being, but they were endlessly (and inadvertently) putting prospects in the Not OK chair with their "I know more than you do" attitude. They didn't mean to, but subject-matter experts often can't help showing off — especially when they're tasked with going into the marketplace and announcing their solution's awesomeness.

One day, this "seller" was in a prospect's office. This prospect was describing their complex in-house solution, which they'd painstakingly patched together to fix the problem (and which our client's solution could solve much more efficiently). Their DIY approach had taken a lot of work, and they were reasonably proud of their accomplishment. But our seller, ever the curious subject-matter expert, couldn't resist asking: "Why did you build it like that?"

Can you hear the derision and condescension in the voice? The prospect did. She ended the conversation immediately. She then called Premium Software to say, "If that seller ever comes back on the premises of my organization, I will call security to escort him out."

Don't ask your prospect why they did something. You probably don't need to know anyway. But if it is essential for you to know why, then soften your language by asking instead: "Please help me understand ..."

"Please help me understand what's driving ..."
"Please help me understand what's behind ..."
"Please help me understand the reasons for ..."

Don't ask why.

COMMUNICATION KEY 5
Ask One Question at a Time

Great sellers ask business-appropriate questions that may make the prospect slightly uncomfortable. These questions help them identify problems and articulate systems or processes in their business that may be deficient or flawed. There is so much potential for discomfort here! (This is why staying in the Not OK chair is so critical.)

I often watch salespeople in role-plays do a great job of using the concept of Recognize + Respond and asking strategic, Open-Ended Questions ... but then they keep asking questions! They don't stop at just one.

It might sound like this:

> *"Our clients tell us we help them lower production costs by as much as 20%. How are you with production costs? Like, what if we could help you lower yours? Would that have any interest for you?"*

There are three questions there! And the last one is a closed-ended question! This example may sound silly, but we've seen countless salespeople ask compound questions just like this.

There is a VERY strong temptation to compound questions — and unfortunately, the piled-on questions tend to be closed-ended. (Notice in my example above, the last question started with, "Would that ... ?") Closed-ended questions will pull you down to the prospect's side of the tracks at Wimp Junction.

Don't overwhelm your prospect with compound questions. Remain in control of the conversation by asking just one strategic question at a time and avoid the temptation to "wimp out" by piling them on and switching to closed-ended questions that feel a little less uncomfortable to ask.

COMMUNICATION KEY 6
Get Comfortable with Silence

When you ask great Open-Ended Questions, your prospect may need a moment to process the question you just asked them before responding. You will be tempted to fill the silence — most sellers are so naturally engaging that they cannot leave silence unfilled, and they immediately start talking again to fill it. This alienates prospects and pulls the seller down the wrong side of the tracks at Wimp Junction, where more talking leads to a premature pitch. (Prospects hate getting a pitch they didn't ask for!)

Avoid the temptation to fill the silence. After you ask your question, let it remain suspended in the air. If you've done a good job of remaining in their Not OK chair, your prospect is thinking about your question. They'll answer you. (On the other hand, if you've been abrasive or arrogant, then their long, stone-faced silence is probably an open challenge. End the call graciously.)

Be prepared to count to ten in silence after you ask each question. You'll rarely ever make it all the way to ten, but the habit will keep you from filling the silence prematurely and will leave room for your prospect to do all the talking.

COMMUNICATION KEY 7
Follow the 80/20 Rule

Your prospect should be talking for 80% of the call. This means you should be talking no more than 20% of the time. Put that into numbers: For every minute you talk, you should listen to your prospect talking for four minutes.

If you're talking for more than one minute out of every five, then you're at high risk of talking about your solution and slipping into premature pitches, which will land you squarely at Step 2 of Wimp Junction.

To control the conversation so you accomplish your goal on the call (to qualify the opportunity and learn about your prospect's pains in the absence of your DV), you must let your prospect do most of the talking.

From your prospect's perspective, they have other things to do with their time; listening to you talk is at the bottom of the list of things they want to accomplish today. Remember, there's one voice in the world prospects love to hear more than ours, and it's theirs.

The only opinion that matters is theirs. You'll never learn about their pain by talking. You'll learn only by listening. When you follow the 80/20 Rule, your prospect will never feel like they're "being sold to" because they will be too busy talking.

Ask questions, remain consultative, and stay on the right side of the tracks by letting your prospect speak for 80% of the call.

COMMUNICATION KEY 8
Get Past RAS

When we begin working with new clients, we always make sure they understand a term called RAS. Even though RAS is a concept pulled from the field of psychology and not from the field of sales, it is relevant to every sales conversation you'll have in the marketplace.

RAS is an acronym that stands for Reticular Activating System, which is the brain's sorting device. RAS is a primal part of the brain related to our fight-or-flight response; it is constantly sorting information coming in to determine what's important and what's not. Anything determined unimportant or irrelevant will get sorted out and discarded.

RAS is the reason you suddenly start seeing every red sedan on the road when you're in the market for a red sedan. RAS is the reason you can hear your name in a noisy crowd.

The toughest gatekeeper you will encounter is your prospect's RAS.

Sales messages that are seller-centric will get sorted out and discarded by the prospect's RAS because they're irrelevant (so far) to the prospect's world. Your prospect's RAS doesn't care who you are, what you're selling, the story behind your brand, or how you get great results. Unless there's a clearly identified opportunity to achieve or a threat to mitigate, your message will be deemed irrelevant to RAS, and you will get sorted out.

Sales messages that sound salesy (i.e., overconfident) will especially get sorted out and discarded by the prospect's RAS because the arrival of a seller threatens the pain of change (not to mention other pains like annoyance, persistence, and manipulative tactics).

So we have to get past RAS if we want our prospect to even hear us past "hello." We'll do that in two primary ways:

1. Intrigue RAS so you don't get sorted out immediately as irrelevant. Open with a negative comment like, "Maybe I'm calling too early, but ..." This jolts the sorting, and RAS isn't sure what

to do with you — it wonders why you're calling at all. Other comments might sound like, "I may be here too late ..." or, "This may not have happened to you yet, but ..."

Those Negative Opening Comments will buy you a few extra seconds. And as a bonus, they'll keep you in the Not OK chair, which is exactly where you want to be in your prospect's mind.

2. Stay focused on the prospect's pain. RAS wants to neutralize threats, and pain is something to be neutralized. If what you're bringing to the conversation is a nice-to-have, like features, benefits, savings, kitties, rainbows, or unicorns, RAS will sort you out as irrelevant. But if RAS picks up on a pain threat you can alleviate, then it wants to know more.

"This may not have happened to you yet, but we work with executives who aren't fully satisfied with the options being presented to them to avoid [and then you tell a 1-Sentence Story to describe the scenario from hell]."

If you're tuned in to the value your DV really holds for your prospect, then your story will be relevant to your prospect's world; it will resonate with RAS and will buy you enough extra precious seconds of attention to begin engaging your prospect. Conversely, if you talk about yourself or your solution instead of their pain, you'll be sorted out.

COMMUNICATION KEY 9

Know the Culture

Selling is human-to-human interaction. Every great seller must recognize the impact of their prospect's culture on the interaction. This impact could spring from broad cultural differences across countries — for example, business dinners in Mexico will start later, go longer, and require a lot more "small talk" than business dinners in Germany, and a seller must be prepared to adapt their conversational style to fit their prospect's expectations. Similarly, written correspondence in France tends to be more formal than in the United States, and a seller should adjust their outreach messages accordingly.

Business attire will also differ across countries, companies, and industries. If my prospect is a banker in Hong Kong, a conservative suit will improve my rapport and credibility. But if my prospect is a small agricultural manufacturer in the midwestern United States, I can probably leave the suit at home and dress more comfortably to improve my chances of building rapport.

Here's the point: Sellers must put themselves second when it comes to self-expression. This is humility in action. In order to earn our prospect's cooperation and consent to move forward, we must know their culture — even just a few basics — and prioritize their preferences, not ours. Otherwise, we risk inadvertently alienating the humans with whom we're trying to cooperate.

Know the culture of the country, region, industry, or company you're targeting. Take a few minutes to learn it, and plan your engagement accordingly. This doesn't mean being fake when you interact with your prospects; it simply means adapting to honor their cultural preferences over yours as you pursue their business.

COMMUNICATION KEY 10
Soften Your Language

Many salespeople and executives are wonderfully confident human beings who make the marketplace better by speaking with candor. Unfortunately, their blunt directness can inadvertently rankle a prospect and plop them into the Not OK chair, which unnecessarily slows down the cadence of their sales. (It takes more time and work to engage prospects who aren't cooperative, and you need to find more of them!)

We've worked with over ten thousand salespeople from more than two thousand companies. Many were already elite sellers before they came to us. They were experts in their industry and knew their solutions inside and out. They had effective processes. But they'd plateaued in their efforts and wanted to figure out how to break into the next level of success. Of all the enhancements they learned from us, this one — softening their language — lifted everything else for them.

Softening your language doesn't mean you soften your backbone; your goal is still to ruthlessly qualify your opportunity. It simply means you allow your prospect (the other human being) to be comfortable enough in the conversation to continue cooperating with you.

Remember, our goal is to extend the conversation so we can collect information to determine if this is an opportunity worth pursuing — and we can only do that with the prospect's cooperation. Most salespeople have room to soften their language with small changes in nuance, tone, and wording. This helps them come across as less abrasive and earns the cooperation of their prospects faster.

While the concept may sound great, it's a little abstract. Let me share some concrete examples here for guidance. They may not all specifically apply to you, but please use them to find areas of your own language that might sound a bit abrasive or arrogant without intending to, and soften them similarly.

Asking questions that call the prospect incompetent

One time, we started working with a wonderful client we'll call Brokerage, Inc. who wisely taught the salespeople on their team to ask questions — a LOT of questions — on their sales calls. Brokerage, Inc. understood the importance of asking over telling (a great start!), but unfortunately, their questions still weren't getting them a lot of traction in the marketplace.

After one round of role-plays, we quickly understood why.

Brokerage, Inc.'s salespeople were simply using the questions to point out how incompetent their prospects were. *"Did you know ... [insert here: some version of 'you've been doing it wrong without us']?"*

Never mind that "Did you" is a closed-ended question. The bigger problem is that the only possible answers are: (a) a fight ("Yes, I DID know") or (b) the Not OK chair ("No, I must be an idiot! Thanks for pointing it out!").

When you ask questions, you must make sure you're not accidentally using them as a tool to call your prospect incompetent.

Even with Open-Ended Questions, the temptation is still strong to point out how the prospect has been doing it wrong:

> *"When you looked at how outdated and inefficient your current systems are, what did you find?"*

Listen to your own questions and make any modifications necessary to edify your prospect so you don't inadvertently call them incompetent.

We regularly get solicited by salespeople as they call on small business owners. One email went straight to the point: "I'm a website expert, and I found eighty-seven different problems with your website. Did you know you're missing out on hundreds of valuable leads every day? Call me and I'll show you how we can find them."

This seller had no idea we'd just finished our website overhaul with expensive professional help, and they weren't exactly building a bridge to our goodwill by calling it a mess. (Spoiler alert: We didn't respond.)

It's too easy to make the prospect feel insulted by asking an edgy question unintentionally. Take care to ensure you're putting your prospects in the OK chair with the questions you ask.

Not giving your prospect enough credit

One of the easiest ways to put your prospect in the OK chair is by giving them credit for the efforts they expended before you walked into the room.

Too often we hear sellers announce their presence with something like, "Thank goodness my solution is here! You've been failing without me!" The prospect quickly (and correctly) surmises that the seller has absolutely no idea what's going on in their world, and dismisses them.

If you want to earn your prospect's engagement, soften your language by giving them credit. In our line of business, for example, we don't just help clients lift top-line revenues and bolster margins. We help clients lift top-line revenues and bolster margins ... *beyond what they've been able to accomplish thus far.*

This isn't a cheap manipulation tactic — it's the absolute truth. Your prospects have been whacking at the problem you solve, and you cannot walk in arrogantly assuming you bring divine inspiration out of the blue. Strike a humbler tone and give them credit for (a) being aware of the problem you solve and (b) already taking a stab at solving it. This keeps them in the OK chair, indicates your awareness of their world, and earns their cooperation faster.

I don't understand → I'm not sure I understand

A hallmark of the Slattery method is the simple little phrase, "I'm not sure I understand." This sentence allows you to volley the ball of conversation back over the net, where your prospect will return it with more clarity. This extends the conversation so you can get the information you need.

Here's an example:

Let's say your prospect declares, *"We need lower prices."*

A rookie salesperson might scramble back into the OK chair with, *"Yeah, but our value ..."*

> Or, the rookie salesperson might roll over with, *"I'll see what I can do!"*

> A great seller will seek further clarity: *"I'm not sure I understand."*

That simple phrase softly lobs the ball back over the net, allowing your prospect to clarify what they mean by "lower prices" — after all, those words will mean different things to different people. The conversation continues toward clarity with the prospect's cooperation.

When we start working with sales teams, many experienced sellers quickly grasp the concept but miss the nuance, and they instead say abrasively, "I don't understand."

Run a role-play with a colleague and try saying, "I don't understand," softly. It's impossible. It's a passive-aggressive way of saying, "I don't get it — why are you being so dumb?"

So instead of saying the abrasive phrase, "I don't understand" (or worse, "I don't get it"), carefully keep your language gentle with the softer, "I'm not sure I understand."

It's a small change, but it makes a huge difference.

Pacing → Slow down

In our modern-day knowledge economies, we place a premium on having the right answers, knowing a lot, and answering questions quickly.

Unfortunately, these tactics backfire in sales, the one area of any economy where quick-speaking "I know more than you do" answers will sabotage any efforts to do business.

When selling, it's critical to keep the other human being comfortably seated in the OK chair. The pacing of your voice affects the tone of the conversation. When we want to show off our knowledge (and put the prospect in the Not OK chair), we speak quickly. But to keep our prospects OK, we probably need to slow down a bit. This doesn't mean speaking like a sloth — rather, it means being aware of your pacing to match that of your prospect, and resisting the temptation to accelerate.

Be especially aware of the temptation to accelerate your speech when prospects push back. Speaking faster is a natural response to pressure. Unfortunately, this acceleration escalates the conversation up a notch. It may not quite be a confrontation, but it's definitely uncomfortable, and the prospect can sense it.

Keeping a slower pace when speaking will help you avoid the sense of escalation that might otherwise occur in your selling conversations and will help you remain nonconfrontational.

Volume → Lower it

When we feel confident and knowledgeable, we speak loudly. Try lowering your volume. This may seem counterintuitive, since sellers have been taught for decades to exude confidence. Unfortunately, this can come across as brash arrogance in the marketplace. A sale already begins with the assumption that we know more than the prospects do; announcing this confidently won't win prospects' cooperation — it will only make them less OK, and thus less likely to engage.

To help win their engagement, take care to lower your volume a few notches in conversations. You don't need to be difficult to hear, just humble. Simply lower your voice from announcing, "I'm amazing, and I know more than you!" to, "Let's have a conversation."

The quieter volume will help you avoid seeming overeager too. Prospects can sense a hungry salesperson with dollar signs in their eyes. Such eagerness puts the salesperson at risk of alienating the prospect or, worse, appearing more committed than the prospect is to solving their problem, which makes them more vulnerable to requests, discounts, and concessions.

Keep your voice soft and conversational. It will help you stay in commitment rapport with your prospect.

Terry is so effective at this skill that when we filmed him for our online training modules during the COVID-19 shutdown in 2020, our team had trouble picking up his voice on multiple microphones, all set to maximum input. His voice automatically softens and tones down as soon as he gets into this stuff. It makes him ruthlessly effective in sales conversations, where prospects feel good, cooperate willingly, answer his questions voluminously, and get to clarity around their pain with shocking speed.

ME → Negative Opening Comment

When introducing ourselves to prospects in the marketplace, it's tempting to transparently announce our name, our company, and what we sell: "I'm Jennica Dixon, and I'm calling from the Acme Corporation!" While this disclosure may feel open and honest, it can inadvertently sabotage our selling efforts. This is because it's completely focused on us (and is probably even delivered with some measure of rapport-killing "I'm awesome!" confidence).

The prospect doesn't care about who we are, our last name, where we're calling from, what company we work for, or what we sell. If we open with those lines, we will sound like every other overconfident seller announcing their untimely arrival into the prospect's world. The prospect will tune out.

Instead, we must be entirely focused on the prospect. Every moment of their day matters; they don't want to spend precious seconds listening to us talk about ourselves.

So instead of opening the conversation with some kind of statement about us, we recommend opening it with what we call the Negative Opening Comment: a simple self-effacing statement of humility and honesty that can earn another moment of your prospect's valuable time and keep them in the OK chair.

It might sound like this:

> *"I may be calling too early ..."*
> *"This may not have happened to you yet ..."*
> *"I may not have ended up at the right number ..."*

This simple tactic shifts the focus from you to your prospect. It puts you solidly in the Not OK chair so your prospect can comfortably engage with you. It also helps you get past your prospect's RAS because you won't fit into the typical sorting patterns, and RAS will need to hear just a bit more to figure out how to sort you.

Simply follow the Negative Opening Comment with an Open-Ended Question that's totally focused on the prospect (not you), and your chances of having a real conversation with them go up astronomically.

CHAPTER SEVEN

Engage – Part 2

The Prospect's Buying System

STEP 1
*The prospect lies
to the salesperson.*

STEP 2
*The prospect gets the
salesperson to provide
valuable information
and a quote.*

STEP 3
*The prospect lies
about what's going
to happen next.*

STEP 4
*The prospect doesn't
answer or return the
salesperson's calls.*

Your System

STAGE 1
Differentiate

STAGE 2
Target

STAGE 3
Engage

STAGE 4
Commit

STAGE 5
Secure

STRATEGIC

Is This a Qualified Selling Opportunity?

Complex sales leave a lot of room for subjective sales forecasting.

We've often heard salespeople announce with confidence, "It's in the bag! They'll make a decision this week!" only to see the deal evaporate. The greatest complaint we hear from CFOs is, "We can't trust our sales forecast."

Without a trustworthy sales forecast, an enterprise can't allocate limited resources to the right places; resources get tied up for prospects who are "thinking it over." Leaders can't make well-informed strategic decisions around production, inventory, or hiring. Bankers can't determine the ongoing financial health of the enterprise. A fiction-free sales forecast is critical to a company's existence.

A fiction-free forecast is built by tracking each sales opportunity through a few simple Attributes, starting with actionable pain. Does this prospect organization have enough pain to justify going through the pain of change? This requires discernment: You may talk to one player in the cast of characters who wants a problem solved, but the organization as a whole doesn't have enough enterprise pain to counter internal resistance to the pain of change.

You want to uncover enough actionable pain at the enterprise to indicate that your sale has a chance of success. We're out to separate the intellectually curious from the economically serious prospects. Ruthless honesty will keep you from presenting an offer to do business to unqualified prospects and getting Think It Overs and ugly surprises. (Your CFO will thank you!)

In order to achieve a solidly bankable sales forecast, you need to ask yourself one hard question about every prospective or current opportunity, and it's this:

Do I really have a Qualified Selling Opportunity here?

In the absence of a clear checklist of Attributes, it's difficult to tell if you have a real opportunity to win the business. In fact, it's difficult to tell where you are in the sale, let alone the likelihood of closing it.

You need to be able to discern a qualified opportunity (one you can win) from an unqualified one. Don't spend your time and resources pitching until you know you have a true Qualified Selling Opportunity (QSO), or you'll land on the prospect's side of the tracks at Wimp Junction.

A QSO is an opportunity you've determined you can win at an acceptable level of commitment of your time and resources. This clarity is accomplished by collecting the Attributes of a QSO in your conversations with the various players in the cast of characters at your prospect organization and waiting to present an offer to do business until all Attributes have been collected.

This requires clear metrics, situational awareness, honesty, humility, and patience. When you can skillfully assess a QSO, the accuracy of your sales forecasts will improve significantly.

As we discussed in the previous chapter, your sales calls have one purpose: to extend the conversation and determine if this is an opportunity worth pursuing. Your time and resources are limited, and once you determine an opportunity isn't worth pursuing, you will be free to pursue others that are.

On your sales calls with various players in the cast of characters at your prospect organization, you'll be collecting the Attributes of a QSO so you know exactly where you are in your sales process. At the same time, you'll be skillfully engaging your prospects with questions that prompt an awareness that things could be different or better. These conversations will help tilt the scale in your favor as the pain and consequences of the status quo pile up in their minds, and the cost of delay becomes the driving force in accelerating your sale.

Call Flow to Collect Attributes

We will share with you the Slattery steps to efficiently collect the Attributes of a QSO. These steps, which we call the Call Flow process, provide an outline for your individual sales conversations so you can collect the Attributes of a QSO. In that sense, these steps provide a "micro" outline for the flow of your sales calls to help you collect the Attributes.

But these Call Flow steps also provide an outline for the whole opportunity as you track exactly which Attributes you've collected so far in your conversations with the various players in the cast of characters. In that sense, these steps provide a "macro" outline, too, for your sales forecast.

In your conversations, you'll traverse the Last Mile of the sale, where marketing cannot go. This is where you'll translate your DV to your prospect's world and maintain their goodwill so you can extend the conversation and determine if this is an opportunity worth pursuing.

This Engage stage carries a high risk of getting diverted to Wimp Junction. Because you're interacting with prospects so much, there are many opportunities for them to pull you over to their side of the tracks. They may try to convince you that you have no DV and should continue down the tracks of their buying system instead, where you'll be commoditized and lose your margins. Maintain high situational awareness here and follow the steps to continue moving forward toward closure.

What this Call Flow Accomplishes for Your Prospect

As you follow the steps of the Call Flow we teach, you'll be gently helping your prospect move from No Pain ("Everything's fine without you!") to an awareness that things could be different or better, to being concerned about the pain, to being committed to fixing the pain.

Remember the scale in your prospect's mind that we discussed in Chapter 4? This scale teeters between the pain of change and the pain of staying the same (the pain of not having your DV). Your goal, with your skillfully-asked questions, is to help your prospect weigh down the scale in their mind on the side of staying the same (not having your DV) until it outweighs the pain of change, and they're committed to fixing the pain.

It looks like this in their mind:

none
aware
CONCERNED
COMMITTED

However, please notice something very important: Their commitment is not to buy anything from you! They're simply committed to fixing their pain. They haven't yet seen the solution — and we don't present our solution or an offer to do business until we're absolutely certain (i.e., we've heard it come out of their mouths) that they're committed to fixing the pain.

It takes valuable time and resources to present our solution or an offer to do business to a prospect; therefore, we only want to be presenting to those prospects who have real motivation to change and who are committed to alleviating their pain.

If we present our solution before they commit to alleviating their pain, then we'll get a Think It Over at Wimp Junction, where we'll end up as column fodder on a spreadsheet.

This process is intended to help you gather information so you can qualify your opportunity and help your prospect go down the funnel in their own mind from "No pain!" to "When can this be fixed?"

Funnel to Clarity

As you engage your prospects throughout this process, you will encounter our No-Fail Selling Rule #4: Prospects lie with ambiguous, conditional words. Accept none of them.

Some prospects may appear to be polite or even enthusiastic about what you're selling; do not mistake these signals for legitimate green lights to start pitching.

Prospects have every incentive to get you talking so that you provide valuable information and Unpaid Consulting at Wimp Junction. They will feign interest, lying with vague, ambiguous, conditional words like *value, partner, better, less expensive, faster, lower cost, commodity, common, table stakes, interested,* and *"We'll get back to you soon."*

Prospects use broad, vague, ambiguous, conditional words and phrases for various reasons: to keep you talking (while you provide valuable information); to keep you at arm's length (where you'll never win the sale); to avoid facing the pain of change (which your sale would necessarily bring).

NO-FAIL RULE #4
Prospects lie with ambiguous, conditional words.
Accept none of them.

The key to moving your sale forward on your side of the tracks at Wimp Junction is clarity. There must be clarity between you and your prospect.

Clarity will allow you to qualify your opportunities faster. The prospect may say they need the problem fixed "right away" — but what does right away really mean? Does it mean they're willing go through the pain of change today? Next week? Fifth quarter next fiscal year?

You'll be tempted to "wimp out" and let them get away with ambiguities, but you must stay the course and funnel them down to clarity so you can determine whether or not you have a Qualified Selling Opportunity.

Getting clarity around ambiguous words will also help your prospect process and articulate the pains they're experiencing in the absence of your DV. This is where your selling skills will be truly consultative. Your prospect-centric, Open-Ended Questions will bring them to an awareness that things could be different or better; your further questions to clarify their answers will help them identify more specifically the costs and consequences they're currently experiencing, and articulate the pain of the status quo. Getting to clarity around these topics will be tremendously helpful to your prospects; ambiguity is not in their best interest.

Our language has hundreds of thousands of words, and we combine them to describe complex, conceptual, and abstract topics like, "return on investment." Words have multiple possible meanings, and context can change everything. Because of this, it usually takes multiple verbal exchanges back and forth to intentionally reach clarity.

This brings us to No-Fail Selling Rule #5: The truth and the money for me only come with clarity.

Memorize this phrase: *"The truth and the money for me only come with clarity."*

NO-FAIL RULE #5
The truth and the money for me
only come with clarity.

These words are critical to helping you remember that you cannot win on ambiguity — you must funnel your prospect's ambiguous words down to clarity. This usually takes multiple verbal exchanges back and forth.

For example, a prospect might tell us that our price is "too high." But ... what does too high mean? Everyone has their own internal gauge that beeps and flashes when something's too expensive, but everybody's gauge is calibrated to a different amount. Sellers often jump to defending their solution before getting clarity on what the prospect actually means.

We must stay prospect-centric and continue asking questions to get to the tightest clarity possible.

WE ASK A QUESTION

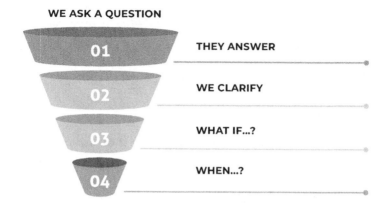

01   **THEY ANSWER**

02   **WE CLARIFY**

03   **WHAT IF...?**

04   **WHEN...?**

When they tell us we seem too expensive, ask for clarity gently, using the principle of Recognize + Respond: *"We get that a lot. Please help me understand what 'too high' means in this case."*

They may respond with another ambiguity, like: "We need to keep our costs down, and your competitor is half that amount."

Another Recognize + Respond will get you closer to clarity: *"That makes a lot of sense; we tend to look higher when price is the only number on the table. I have to ask — what if it turned out that we could lower overall business costs on the production side?"*

"Well, that would be intriguing."
"You're an astute professional, and I imagine there's a pretty high bar to interest you. Please help me understand what kind of production cost reduction would intrigue you."

"Twenty percent, no less."

"Ehh, that's not too bad. When your incumbent provider was last here for their quarterly site visit and you told them you might want that, what was their response?"

"Um ... we haven't yet."

"Well, you're busy and have a lot to juggle. If it turned out you could get more than a 20% cost reduction on the production side, when would you want to know?"

**We ask a Question
and they answer**

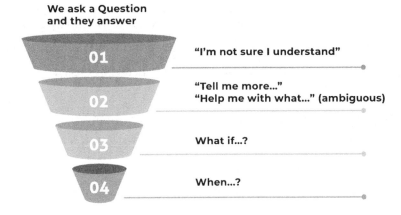

01   **"I'm not sure I understand"**

02   **"Tell me more..."**
"Help me with what..." (ambiguous)

03   **What if...?**

04   **When...?**

Why this funnel is key

It may sound like this funnel is just another step in a selling system, but at Slattery, it's *every step* in our system.

As you engage your prospects in conversation on your sales calls, you'll funnel their answers down to clarity at every step before moving forward.

That's why it's critical that you understand and master this funnel. If you can master the funnel, you can master this way of selling.

TACTICAL: *Call Flow 1–6*

Let's get to the heart of our sales process execution: Call Flow. Call Flow is a term we use to describe the orderly progression through the steps of your sales calls to collect the Attributes of a Qualified Selling Opportunity (QSO), one by one.

If you follow the flow we teach you here, you'll collect the Attributes and determine whether or not you do, in fact, have a QSO worth pursuing. Step by step, Attribute by Attribute, you collect the answers you need and funnel them down to clarity.

Call Flow is a consistent process to fully qualify an opportunity before you provide a quote or proposal because a fully qualified opportunity brings a significantly higher win rate. Call Flow is how we separate the intellectually curious from the economically serious prospects and reach 90% win rates.

In this chapter, we'll teach you the first six Call Flow steps. We're saving the last three Call Flow steps for the Commit stage. By the time we're done, you will know whether or not you have a fully qualified opportunity and can present your solution and an offer to do business.

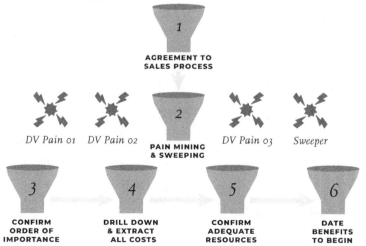

1 — AGREEMENT TO SALES PROCESS

DV Pain 01   DV Pain 02   2 — PAIN MINING & SWEEPING   DV Pain 03   Sweeper

3 — CONFIRM ORDER OF IMPORTANCE   4 — DRILL DOWN & EXTRACT ALL COSTS   5 — CONFIRM ADEQUATE RESOURCES   6 — DATE BENEFITS TO BEGIN

The funnel shapes are not an accident; they are reminders to be patient in achieving clarity. You will use the Funnel to Clarity again and again, until you have the clarity you need. Then, and only then, will you proceed to the next step, and collect the next QSO Attribute.

The order of these steps is intentional. We don't recommend jumping around and asking questions out of order because you may not get the answers you need from your prospect.

You might be able to accomplish all of these Call Flow steps in one or two conversations, or it might take you more. You'll become faster as you practice, but speed is not the goal — clarity is. Stay relaxed, control the call, and keep the prospect in the OK chair as you collect the answers you need.

Call Flow Step 1: *Agreement to the sales process*

This first step is a critical action that many salespeople inadvertently miss: We ask the prospect to agree to the sales process without literally asking them to do it. We need their cooperation and consent every step of the way, and it's too easy to jump into our sales process without asking for their agreement to move forward. Getting their agreement here buys you their goodwill and increases their willingness to engage; they don't feel like they're being sucked into a sales pitch.

This step also strategically and subtly positions you to avoid being commoditized later. The fact that you're asking for their agreement to move forward means you must be comfortable getting no for an answer — which means you aren't desperate for this business. Desperate salespeople can be pressured for discounts and concessions. You can't.

The whole sales process involves you and the prospect exploring a solution that can help fix their pain, and it costs you time and resources. This process requires equal commitment from you and your prospect. Never become more committed than the prospect is to fixing their problems, or it will leave you vulnerable to commoditization pressures.

In this first step, you'll simply open up your sales call in a way that allows you to move forward and begin collecting the Attributes of a Qualified Selling Opportunity. Your successful opening conversation with the prospect will have these elements:

- You describe the selection process you use to identify an ideal customer that you think you might be able to help.
- You recognize that they may not want to change and that at this point it may appear not worth changing.
- You ask permission to ask some questions to understand if the things you do well would have benefits that would warrant going through the pain of change.
- If it looks like the benefits of change are not worth the effort, the dialogue will end.
- If it looks like the benefits are worth the effort, you will mutually decide the next steps.

Here is an example:

> *"We haven't worked together in the past, but we know that in our world we occasionally help our customers hit home runs. We do very well in certain areas, [describe]. May I ask you a few questions about what issues you're having in those areas?"*

> *(Or, "How open are you to a conceptual discussion on possible enhancements/improvements in those areas?")*
>
> *"If we find out I'm here too early, we'll usually recognize that at the same time, and I'll move on."*

At this step, you're looking for clarity regarding their commitment to going through the sales process, but you're not literally asking them to commit to the sales process. Don't even announce that you have a process. Instead, simply ask permission to ask questions.

WHY THIS STEP IS IMPORTANT

It is important to gain your prospect's agreement to the sales process because you must keep No-Fail Selling Rule #6 at the top of your mind the entire time:

Whenever the prospect asks you to do anything that involves expenditure of your resources, know exactly what will happen next before you do anything.

You and your company have limited resources and other sales to pursue. Don't expend anything (including time and information) without knowing how it will affect your prospect's decision-making process.

NO-FAIL RULE #6

Whenever the prospect asks you to do anything that involves expenditure of your resources, know exactly what will happen next before you do anything.

At this step, you're helping your prospect understand a critical point: that exploring a solution to fix their pain involves the expenditure of your resources and theirs.

The clear agreement at this step must be that as you proceed, if it seems to make no sense for the parties to continue to expend their resources, you will have to walk away. This clarity will help you maintain your boundaries later (and avoid slipping into Unpaid Consulting), and it may even relieve your prospect to know that you won't be around forever.

Of course, you need to be able to say that to the prospect in a way that maintains open and professional communication in future conversations. If it looks like this isn't going to go anywhere now, depart on good terms by taking the Not OK chair and making everything your fault: "It looks like I may be here too early; that's my mistake."

Call Flow Step 2: *Pain mining and sweeping*

In Step 2, we begin mining for all the pains the prospect is experiencing because they do not have your Differentiating Value (DV) in their life. The goal is to get as many pains on the table as you can possibly collect, without offering to fix any of them. On a micro level, we're mining for the pains this individual is experiencing without your DV; but on a macro level, we're also putting together a picture of the enterprise pains that this prospect organization is experiencing without your DV.

This step takes some self-control. It's incredibly easy to hear your prospect describe one pain and immediately launch into a premature pitch about how your solution can fix that problem. We're not yet presenting anything — instead, our goal here is to get multiple pains on the table.

Complex sales can take a long time to conduct, and a lot can change at your prospect organization in that time. People retire; business lines merge; acquisitions are made. If you rest your selling efforts on just one line of pain, then you might lose momentum later when that pain gets buried in various changes. But if you can get three or more enterprise pains on the table now, it will be a lot easier to maintain your forward cadence later. Sales cycles accelerate when sellers get multiple pains on the table earlier. So in this step, you'll start with an opening question and begin mining for at least three pains.

DV Pain 01   DV Pain 02   **PAIN MINING & SWEEPING** 2   DV Pain 03   Sweeper

THE OPENING QUESTION

You'll ask a strategic opening question that leverages your DV and allows you to begin mining for your prospect's pains. There are three opening-question formats we teach at Slattery to put your DV into play. These three formats are the package to carry the "Aha!" message to the prospect that not having your DV may have real consequences to them.

Each of these three opening-question formats takes into account the fact that you are a human being dealing with another human, using the Communication Keys described in Chapter 6. Each format can work in nearly every situation, but there's usually one that's the better fit.

All three formats begin with a Negative Opening Comment, like "I might be here too early, but ..." or "We may not need to talk, but ..."

As we discussed in Chapter 6, this Negative Opening Comment

puts your prospect in the OK chair and interrupts your prospect's Reticular Activating System (which otherwise sorts out overconfident salespeople). This will help you earn and keep their goodwill to continue the conversation.

However, a quick word of caution here: When you choose a Negative Opening Comment for your opening question, be careful to not unintentionally talk down to your prospect by using the phrase, "This may not be important to you." The "to you" is too accusatory. A more effective version might sound like this: "This may not be a priority."

In Format 1, you would follow that Negative Opening Comment with a very short (single-sentence) 1-Sentence Story that is likely to resonate with your prospect's pain(s) in order to determine whether they do, in fact, have the pain your DV can solve.

FORMAT 1

Negative Opening Comment	One-Sentence Story	+ Open-Ended Question
This may not have happened to you yet...	*But one of the most frequent conversations we have is around...*	*What have you seen?*
I may be bringing this up too early/late...		*What have you experienced?*
		How often...?
	But many times when having a converstion... they describe...	*When...?*
		Who...?
		Where...?

The 1-Sentence Story in the middle of your question accomplishes three things:

1. It builds your credibility by showing that you do this a lot in the marketplace — you've seen this before. And it accomplishes this without announcing, "I know more than you do!"

2. It keeps your prospect OK by validating their experience in the marketplace. You're affirming that they're not alone in having this problem.
3. It talks about people like your prospect without talking directly about your prospect. This keeps your prospect OK by affirming they're not incompetent for having this problem — other executives like them also face this issue.

Remember, no one wants a salesperson to walk in and announce, "Hey, you've been doing it wrong!" But they pay a lot of money to hear consultants say, "We've seen a lot of this in the marketplace."

And of course, always end with an Open-Ended Question. Your Format 1 opening question might sound like this:

> *"I may be bringing this up too early, but one of the most frequent conversations we're having in the marketplace with executives at your level is around bolstering their margins beyond what they've been able to achieve so far in their revenue growth. How satisfied are you with margins during your growth?"*

Format 1 is the most useful of the three formats. Use it frequently — it gets your value across.

In Format 2, you would follow that Negative Opening Comment with an assumption about benefits, behaviors, or results that they're probably not experiencing in the absence of your DV — but your question assumes that they are. This question opens up a gap in your prospect's mind, making room for your DV that "telling" never can.

FORMAT 2

Negative Opening Comment	One-Sentence Story	+ Open-Ended Question
We may not need to spend any time on this...	*When you... /* *The last time you...*	*What happened?* *What did you see...?*
This isn't always a priority, but...	*Considered...* *Evaluated...* *Asked...* *Met with...* *Had your monthly...*	*What changed...?* *What was the result...?* *What have you experienced?*

This gap, between what ought to be happening and what's really happening, opens up an awareness of your potential DV in their mind much more effectively than announcing what you offer.

Let's say you're in financial services, and ongoing consultative risk assessments are part of your DV. If you simply announce, *"We offer great risk assessment services,"* your prospect may reply, *"We already get great service, thanks, bye."*

So to open up their awareness that things could be different or better, you might ask them about the quarterly visits their current broker must surely be making (but which they most certainly aren't):

> *"We may not need to spend any time on this, but when your broker came by for their most recent quarterly site visit, what was the result of their risk assessment?"*

Format 2 is most useful when the prospect is currently doing business with your competitor. You're innocently bringing up gaps in service. Use Format 2 when you have an entrenched competitor.

In Format 3, you would follow that Negative Opening Comment with a 1-Sentence Story that raises two potential pains your prospect may be experiencing in the absence of your DV, which they've perhaps never even considered before. Then, you'd ask them to rate which is the greater concern by asking a Two-Choice Question, which prompts a choice between the two options presented.

FORMAT 3

Negative Opening Comment	One-Sentence Story	+ Forced-Choice Question
I'm never sure which may be more important...	*But often when speaking with...* *One of two concerns quickly surfaces: The first is... and the second is...*	*Which of those is the greater concern in this selection/decision?*

> *"I'm never sure which may be more important, but often when speaking with executives at your level, one of two concerns quickly surfaces. The first is the up-front price, and the second is the overall cost of the solution. Which of those is the greater concern in this selection?"*

Format 3 is best when you're talking to someone who's busy because the Two-Choice Question puts two DV points into play at once. Use it when you're in front of a time-pressed Emotional Customer.

However, a word of caution: When you deploy Two-Choice Questions, it's very easy to slip into a "trap close," when the prospect feels like you're trapping them into agreeing with your premises. Jumping straight to a question like, "Will price or cost be more important to you here?" can come across as manipulative, especially if they haven't agreed to the premise that they're in the market for a solution at all. They'll especially shut down if you don't soften it (with a Negative Opening Comment and a 1-Sentence Story), or if your delivery is too fast or assertive.

Check out the difference between these two questions:

Version 1, Aggressive: *"So when you're looking at solutions like ours, is price or cost more important to you?"*

Version 2, Intentional: *"I may be bringing this up too early, but often when speaking with executives who run enterprise technology, the conversation quickly goes to one of two concerns: The first is the up-front price, and the second is the total cost. Which of those is the greater concern for you here?"*

If you stay humble, these questions are marvelously effective and respectful of your impatient prospect's time.

Grab a pen and craft these three questions using the DV points you identified in Chapter 4. You may have to try a few different variations before you have three solid questions you're comfortable using to open conversations with new prospects.

These questions are assets you'll use over and over again in your opening conversations. Ask them gently from the Not OK chair and listen to your prospect answer with the pains they're experiencing because they're not currently your customer.

COMMON MISTAKES

When running this exercise with salespeople in person, we inevitably hear some mistakes in application. Salespeople are so accustomed to "telling" that even when they're forced, as here, to shift over to asking questions, they build their questions so they can stay in the OK chair and tell the prospect how they've been "doing it wrong."

Here are a few of the most common mistakes when salespeople craft questions to leverage their DV and open up a conversation:

- ◆ Using closed-ended questions: anything prompting a yes-or-no answer
  - Beware the closed-ended questions! It's remarkably easy to slip into asking "Could we" or "Would you" here.
  - Asking closed-ended questions will derail your conversation before it even gets rolling. Your prospect will answer with a quick-and-easy yes or no, thus fulfilling any requirement they had to keep the conversation rolling.
  - I've often heard salespeople craft great openings with the Negative Opening Comment and 1-Sentence Story, then ask something like, "Is that a priority for you at this time?"
  - Remember, the person asking questions (and doing just 20% of the talking) is the one who's really in control of the conversation. Ask Open-Ended Questions to listen and learn.

- ◆ Interrogating your prospect: anything starting with the word "Why?"
  - Don't make your prospect justify their answers to you. Always start with Who, What, When, Where, or How.

- ◆ Inadvertently taking a shot at the prospect
  - Sometimes salespeople just can't avoid telling from the OK chair, and they build their questions to not-so-subtly tell the prospect how poorly they're handling everything without their DV.
  - The result is something that takes a shot at the prospect:

"This probably isn't important to you, but when you considered [that you're doing something obviously wrong], what was the result?"

- Don't word your questions to imply that whatever the prospect is currently doing without you is wrong. Remember that in their eyes, they were doing just fine before you came along. Even if they are aware of pain, they're not committed to fixing it with you; you haven't earned that right with them yet. And you'll never earn the right to do business with them if they feel stupid in your presence.

- These "shot" questions are usually a symptom of not having done the DV homework. If you do your homework and dig into the DV you really can bring to this prospect, you'll have enough rich language, entirely focused on their world, to insert into these questions that will help you come across as knowledgeable and consultative, not salesy or insulting.

- To test your language, pretend you're the prospect. Enlist a colleague to ask you the questions you've crafted. Do they make you sneer? Do they trigger any defensiveness in you? Do they hit any nerves? If so, you probably didn't craft them graciously enough. The goal here isn't to hit the prospect over the head or make them feel incompetent; the goal is to open the conversation so the prospect talks freely to you about life without your DV. This requires humility and nuance. If your questions aren't there yet, go back and revise them until they are.

Once you have at least three good DV questions, practice them until you can ask them in your sleep. Only then will you be able to confidently and naturally put your DV into play with your prospects. In summary, your three questions might sound like this:

Format 1: Negative Opening Comment + 1-Sentence Story + Open-Ended Question (OEQ): *"This may not be an issue for you at this time, but often, in the hundreds of CFO conversations we have in a year, they tell us about [Pain 1]. Where are you with that?"*

Format 2: Negative Opening Comment + Assumption + OEQ: *"We may not need to spend a lot of time on this, but when your current broker comes by for their quarterly review of [Pain 1 dangers], what has been most helpful to reduce your risk exposure?"*

Format 3: Negative Opening Comment + Two-Choice Question: *"I'm not sure if either of these is important enough to discuss. Usually when I'm talking to a firm of your size, the conversation quickly goes to one of two concerns [Pain 1 and Pain 2]. If I were going to bring value to you today, which of those would we focus on?"*

WHAT IF THEY HAVE THE PAIN?

When your prospect answers affirmatively that they do, in fact, have the pain you just mentioned in your question, do not jump to a presentation! It's so tempting to deliver a miniature premature pitch as soon as you hear mention of a pain: "Ah! We can fix that for you!"

As soon as you mention your solution, your prospect will reasonably ask, "And how much will that cost?" Welcome to Wimp Junction.

Resist the temptation to jump to solution here. Your prospect hasn't asked for a pitch — they've just mentioned some pain.

Jumping to solution will lose some of the rapport that you've worked so hard to build and will send you down their side of the tracks at Wimp Junction. Instead, simply recognize their answer and keep mining:

> *"Mm-hmm. I'll make a note of that. Often, when an executive is living with [Pain 1], we find that they're also dealing with [Pain 2]. Where are you with that?"*

Remember, the goal here is to collect at least three different pains. If you only uncover one or two pains, unless they're existential, they probably won't be enough for your prospect enterprise to go through the pain of change to fix. Keep mining so you can get all the pains out on the table and determine if there's enough pain at the enterprise to justify moving forward.

WHAT IF THEY ASK FOR A SOLUTION?

Your prospect may ask you, "Can you fix my problem?" Do NOT say yes, or you'll drive straight down the prospect's side of the tracks at Wimp Junction. Do not jump to a premature pitch (even a teeny-tiny miniature one).

They may sound eager and interested, but Logical Customers lie all the time about their interest to induce salespeople to provide valuable Unpaid Consulting and quotes. You're still collecting the Attributes of a Qualified Selling Opportunity; it's too early for a presentation. Stay committed to the process and keep uncovering all their pains.

Even if the person you're talking to is not lying, and they're genuinely interested in knowing more about your solution, avoid jumping to a pitch — not because you're withholding information for the fun of it, but because in this prospect-centric process, you truly do need more information to answer them thoroughly and appropriately. It sounds like this:

> *"I'm not sure, but I should know soon. May I ask a few more questions for clarity and context?"*

This is the most honest and transparent answer you can possibly offer. You haven't yet learned enough about their world to answer either yes or no with integrity; it's in both parties' best interest for you to keep digging. Get all their pains on the table before moving forward.

END WITH A SWEEPER QUESTION

Your opening questions were wonderfully specific, based on what you assumed (thanks to your pre-call work) your prospect is most likely experiencing in the absence of your DV. But there's a chance they're also experiencing pains you aren't aware of, and you want to get those pains out on the table too. So end this step with a sweeper question to unearth any other pains not yet uncovered:

> *"What else were you hoping we might be able to enhance ... ?"*
> *"What else were you hoping we might be able to enhance on the revenue side of your business?"*
> *"What else were you hoping we might be able to enhance on the production side of your business?"*

Collect their pains and continue listening without telling them how you could solve any of them.

Call Flow Step 3: *Confirm order of importance*

Now that we have the prospect's pains laid out in front of us, we ask them which of the pains they just articulated is most important to them.

It is critical that you maintain a consultative approach to investigating possible solutions. Prior to discussing all the costs of their pains and problems in detail (which you'll do soon), you want to know which ones are most important to them, and in what order.

Don't tell them which pain or problem *you* think is most important because telling isn't selling; besides, your assumption might be wrong. Their priorities might surprise you. In a complex sale, you'll have multiple conversations with various players in the cast of characters, many of whom have different and sometimes competing priorities. You want to know what's most important to each person who will get a vote in this business decision. Don't assume you know what they are for each player.

This question also keeps the selling process prospect-centric. Their priorities are more important than yours in this conversation. This helps keep your prospect OK and engaged. (It will also differentiate you from most of the other sellers who come through their office talking about their awesome solutions.) Here's what it sounds like:

> *"Here are the [pains, problems, concerns] I heard. Is that everything?"*
> *"In what order should we focus on them?"*

Whatever you do, don't ask the prospect, "Why'd you pick that one?" after they tell you which pain is most important. "Why" questions are interrogation. And in this case, it doesn't matter why they picked it; they picked it, move on. If you really want to know, you can Recognize + Respond with something like, *"Sure. Please help me understand the reasons ..."*

We must stay prospect-centric through this whole process. We cannot shift to being seller- or solution-centric. This is about them, not us. Their order of importance matters, not ours.

This information (about what's most important to them) will be critical later as you navigate their evaluation and decision-making process. Keep your notes.

Call Flow Step 4: *Extract all costs by drilling down*

This is a major step. In it, you'll drill down on the pain your prospect just picked as their top-priority problem to fix, and you'll extract all the costs and consequences they're living with because of it.

Here's why: The cost of the problem determines the cost of fixing it.

No-Fail Selling Rule #7 says: If the prospect can't tell you the cost of the problems, they will not spend money to fix them.

NO-FAIL RULE #7
If the prospect can't tell you the cost of the problems,
they will not spend money to fix them.

The prospect must articulate every cost of these problems. They must have a clear understanding of how much it's costing them to miss out on your DV, and no amount of "telling" from a salesperson will get them there.

Remember, prospects don't believe salespeople. They know you're incented to drag them through the pain of change. If you articulate what their problem is costing them, they will fight your number. But if they articulate what their problem is costing them, they'll believe the number.

The only numbers that matter are *theirs*. Until they can articulate the cost of their own pain, they haven't internalized that number, and they won't spend what it costs to fix their problem.

The mere existence of pain won't prompt your prospect to action — they must know what the problems are *currently costing* them. Then, and only then, will they consider spending money to fix them.

So, in this step, you will ask questions to uncover every cost of the problems they're living with.

Listen for vague answers and ambiguous terms, and funnel them down to clarity. No pitches, no telling, no teaching—just a lot of Open-Ended Questions. Remember, "The truth and the money for me only come with clarity." Keep drilling down! Here are examples of questions you might ask at this step:

- *"What would you like to have different or better?"*
  - Let them tell you! Then funnel their answers down to clarity so you understand what their answers mean to them.
- *"How long have you been living with that situation?"*
  - This gives you past-tense pain! Then funnel their answers down to clarity.

- *"How do you measure the impact of that on your business?"*
  - This tells you what metrics they're looking at on their dashboards to measure their pain. Remember this currency and use it in future conversations to stay relevant to their world. And, of course, funnel the answers down to clarity.
- *"What steps have you already taken to deal with it?*
  - This is gold — you want them to tell you all the ways they've already tried to fix the problem. Maybe they tried to build their own solution, or they went with a competitor. Funnel the answers down to clarity.
- *"What results did you get?"*
  - You already know it didn't work or they wouldn't still have the problem, but you want *them* to tell you. You want this information out on the table now, or they'll keep these options in their back pocket as alternatives to your solution when they want to avoid the pain of change later. You want them to articulate that they did not work. Then funnel the answers!
- *"What do you estimate it's costing the business each month?"*
  - *This* is the cost of the status quo — the cost of keeping the problem now. This is also the cost of delay — the cost of keeping the problem longer while they search for a solution. Funnel the answer down to clarity!
  - Other versions include:
    - » *"What is the financial impact of these problems on your business?"*
    - » *"How do you measure the financial impact of these problems?"*
    - » *"What is your estimate of the total cost of these problems on the enterprise?"*

◆ *"What do you plan to do next?"*

- Their honest answer here will give you an idea into their evaluation and decision-making process, which is critical to winning the sale. Of course, funnel the answer down to clarity.

You'll collect these answers for *each of the pains* you pulled out in Step 2, and you'll do it in the order of importance they told you in Step 3.

In other words, you'll get all the information you can about the costs and consequences of the pain they said was their top priority. When you're done, you'll go to their second-priority pain, and run the same drill-down questions to gain full clarity around the costs and consequences of that problem too. And then the third pain (and the fourth, etc., if there are more).

The goal is to extract all the costs and consequences that they've experienced, are currently experiencing, and will experience because they're not our customer.

This step is critical to get your prospect's full "buy-in" to the process and the cost of delay on the table. There are two important points to remember about this step:

1. Remain humble and consultative here. We must ask strategic questions that allow the prospect to articulate the cost of their problems in the absence of our DV, and we must receive their answers gracefully (no pitching!).

2. Our goal here is not to have them declare how much they'll spend with us — that would be too premature! Rather, our goal is simply to have them indicate the amount they're spending *right now with this problem in their lives*. We want the cost of the problem on the table first because that will provide the

right context for the cost of our solution (and the cost of going through the pain of change) later.

When you're at this step and asking these questions to extract the full cost of the problem, you may get a few different types of answers. Anticipate getting the following replies from the prospect:

- "I don't know."
  - (You can respond with: *"That's okay! I'll live with your best guess."*)
- Some form of "I'm not going to tell you."
  - (You can funnel further with: *"I'm not sure I understand."*)

If they won't tell you, you can say: *"It's okay that we can't establish an exact dollar amount. Do you think it's costing the business enough money that it's worth stopping it (or fixing it)?"* or, *"Who'd want to stop it if you don't want to?"*

Be aware that their tight-lipped response may indicate that you're talking to the wrong person. Maintain situational awareness: Are you talking to the Logical Customer or the Emotional Customer?

WHEN YOU'RE TALKING TO THE LOGICAL CUSTOMER

The Logical Customer tends to be isolated from the pain and costs of the problem you're solving; they're reluctant to spend for a solution. They're also price-oriented and immune to the costs of choosing the lowest bidder. They're rewarded for not spending money, even to fix a problem experienced by the Emotional Customer. They'll stall you here while the Emotional Customer (who needed the problem fixed yesterday) will generally engage and answer your questions honestly.

But you may not always have access to the Emotional Customer, so the next best thing is to bring their agenda into any conversation you're having with the Logical Customer (LC). If you do it right, you may get the LC to admit to a certain level of spend to fix the problem.

Ask the LC honest, situationally-appropriate business questions that assume the LC had the courtesy and integrity to inform the Emotional Customers (EC) that in order for the LC to reach their goals, the EC would have to accept lower margins, smaller market share, or whatever other consequences of the LC's agenda. Do use Recognize + Respond, affirming the challenges of their position:

> *"I know you're under tremendous pressure to reduce the prices you pay ..."*

And then use assumptive questions:

> *"I'm curious — when you explained to the brand manager that you're under tremendous pressure to reduce the price you pay for ingredients, and that they'd have to live with lower margins, longer time to market, smaller market share, and smaller top-line revenue, how'd they feel about taking one for the team?"*

This points out their isolation as well as the conflicting agendas between price and cost.

> *"I know you are under tremendous pressure to minimize up-front price. When you explained to [the Emotional Customer] that the lowest price could be the highest cost for the corporation, what was the response?"*

Be very careful to not take a shot at your prospect here. Stay humble, stay in the Not OK chair, and keep your tone gentle. Ask your question honestly.

WHEN YOU'RE TALKING TO THE EMOTIONAL CUSTOMER

Even when you're talking to the Emotional Customer (EC), you'll need to make sure they can articulate the cost of the problem and how much a solution might cost. This is because every company always has more requests for money than money to spend. Your EC will be up against all the other cost centers and expense groups competing to spend limited company dollars. The employee who comes to the table with vague requests will get $0. The employee who can state exactly what problems are being solved and how much those problems are currently costing the company will likely get the amount they're requesting.

This is why it's so important to run this drill-down and ask questions that help your prospect articulate all the costs and consequences they're currently living with because they're not your customer. If they cannot articulate the cost of the problem, they will not spend money to fix it. But if they do articulate the costs and consequences, then they'll be able to defend their internal request for funding later.

QUICK CHECKLIST

Before moving on, it's helpful to check your notes to make sure you know the following points about each of the various pains your prospect said they were living with:

◆ What is the full cost of the pain (past, present, and future)?

- How is the cost measured? (What's the currency? Is it market share? Growth? Customer retention? Production costs? Time to market?)
- Whose dashboard shows the impact of the problem?
- What's been tried already?
- What has the incumbent been doing?

If you don't have robust answers to those questions, you have some room to go back and fill in your notes. Ask more questions and drill down deeper in your next conversation.

Call Flow Step 5: *Confirm adequate resources*

Your prospect just told you how much the problem is costing them. Now, you'll confirm they're actually willing to spend money to fix it, and how much.

There is a lot of nuance here! We're still not talking about our solution, how much it costs, or how much they'll spend with us. That's all too seller-centric. We must remain prospect-centric, or we risk getting ahead of the prospect in our commitment to solving their problem. (And when we get ahead of them, we're out of commitment rapport and vulnerable to pressures for discounts and concessions.) Your questions to confirm adequate resources might sound like this:

> *"When you set expectations internally about what the business was going to have to spend to fix these problems, what did that look like?"*

> *"That's an interesting number. How did you arrive at it?"*

Please remember the most important point at this step: Their resources have nothing to do with the price of your solution! This has nothing to do with your solution at all! We're talking about how much they're ready to spend to fix the problem they just articulated is costing them so much money each month or quarter.

Do not jump to your solution here, no matter how tempting it is. You're still determining if this is a Qualified Selling Opportunity so you can avoid the interminable delays and Unpaid Consulting of Wimp Junction. Besides that, your prospect hasn't yet committed to solving the problem — don't get ahead of them by launching into a pitch they didn't request about how YOU can solve it. At every step, maintain equal commitment rapport with them and respect their pace. Don't get ahead of them.

WHAT IF THEY ASK FOR A PRICE?

At this step, your prospect may naturally ask you about the cost of your solution. Since your solution is being sold by salespeople like you, I assume you can't simply produce a simple pricing sheet from your website and will need further information to give an accurate quote. (If I'm wrong, and you have a simple pricing sheet, then I have to question whether your solution really needs salespeople or if better marketing could accomplish the growth your enterprise is seeking more cost-effectively.)

It's perfectly fine to affirm your prospect's inquiry with a range — but because you don't yet have enough information to give a precise and accurate answer, please ensure your range is wide enough to account for all possible contingencies. Be honest about the wide range:

> *"Based on our conversation thus far, I can give you a range that will account for certain contingencies that may or may not be relevant to you, so it'll probably end up sounding like a quote for an aircraft carrier. Is that okay?"*

(Asking for your prospect's permission before moving forward at each step with little check-in questions like, "Is that okay?" is a way to continually respect their autonomy in the conversation.) They'll probably affirm that a wide range is fine. You'll answer with some self-effacing humor to put yourself in the Not OK chair:

> *"Okay, make sure you're sitting down; when price is the only number on the table, we look really expensive."*

Then put the price range in the context of your clients' results with a short 1-Sentence Story, so you're telling a story more than presenting a number:

> *"Some of our clients who were facing similar problems took a bare-minimum approach and saw [good results] for $X. Others decided to go after the whole thing and got [amazing results that lowered TCOOL, increased their market share, etc.], and they did the full package with us for about $Z. What were you hoping to hear?"*

Naturally, that high number ("$Z" in this example) is still smaller than the results (like revenue lift, ROI, or market share) your clients got in your story because you solved their pain. The story about their results puts your number in the right context.

This is very important: Make sure that even the low end of the range ("$X" in this example) is big enough to account for all possible contingencies. In other words, that lowest number should actually be pretty big — the amount you can reasonably expect this prospect to spend with you if you solve their basic problem.

If your final quote ends up lower than $X, that won't upset your prospect nearly as much as getting a final quote for something higher than $X when they've picked the basic solution. Pad your range so that there are no nasty surprises later because they will cost you credibility and rapport.

Naturally, if $X is big, then $Z will be astronomical. That's okay. This is intentional and honest. You're not competing on price. If your prospect wants to go to the moon, they'll need to buy a rocket ship, not a scooter. Your top-range price puts you in a different league in your prospect's mind than your competitors who are offering the lowest price. You solve different problems.

Your lower number of the range ("X") will help anchor your solution as attainable and should keep your prospect from abandoning the conversation altogether.

However, if you find that your prospect freaks out at your honest price range, then that's a symptom of two potential problems:

1. You're talking to the price-conscious Logical Customer who would freak out at the price even if you were giving your solution away for free because they always do scripted reactions to price announcements.

2. You didn't get the cost of the problem fully on the table in Step 4. It's so important to have the prospect articulate the cost of the problem first! It puts the cost of the solution in context. The order of these steps is intentional. Remember No-Fail Selling Rule #7: If the prospect can't tell you the cost of the problems, they will not spend money to fix them.

THE WORST QUESTION

The worst question to ask at this step is: "What's your budget?" So many salespeople make it this far, miss the nuance, and blow everything by asking, "So, what's your budget to solve this problem?" It's a terrible question. The prospect knows that you're a salesperson who's probably paid some sort of commission, and when you ask that question, you're effectively asking, "How much will I get paid?" It destroys trust and rapport.

Moreover, a "budget" number isn't the same as the amount they're willing to spend to fix this particular problem. If they've never had a skilled salesperson help them overcome isolation and articulate this problem and what it's costing them, then it's possible they have never allocated anything to fix it. But once the costs and consequences are articulated, and they realize they're already funding the problem every day, then they'll find the money to stop the bleed.

Call Flow Step 6: *Draw out the exact date to begin harvesting the benefits of a solution*

You need clarity around their pain calendar as you continue qualifying your opportunity. If they're okay living with this problem for another year, you need to know that. The goal here is to find out when they want their problem to be gone.

Pay attention here: You're not asking when they'll *select a solution!* Rather, you're figuring out when they want their *problem fixed and the benefits flowing to them.* This is about them and their pain, not about you and your solution.

Too often in enterprise sales, we see salespeople (often brilliant subject-matter experts and consultants) go straight to the *I* word: implementation. They're already thinking ahead to how and when this solution will be implemented.

But the prospect hasn't yet agreed to your solution! Talking about when your solution will be implemented is about you, not them, and you're jumping ahead of your prospect. Stay in commitment rapport.

Also, "implementation" is Logical-Customer language; if you use LC language with the Emotional Customer, you risk being sent down the escalator at your prospect organization: "I don't know anything about implementation schedules ... but we've got an engineer who can talk to you about that. Let me give you their number." You'll have trouble getting back up to the strategic elevation you need to sell your value, and you'll be stuck at Wimp Junction. Keep the focus on the prospect. It might sound like this:

> *"When were you hoping to have the new process in place and costs going down?"*

> *"When were you hoping to have the new process in place and sales going up?"*

Notice that we ask when they were hoping to have the problem gone or the pain stopped. Hope is an emotional word that resonates deeply and tends to prompt more honest answers. *"When were you hoping to have the [problem] fixed and the [benefits] flowing?"*

Naturally, their answers will be ambiguous. They'll use vague words, like "soon." Funnel them down to clarity:

> *"'Soon' is one of those words that tends to mean different things to different people. Please help me understand what soon means for you here."*

If they give you a far-out future answer, like "fifth quarter next fiscal year," that means they think they can live with the cost of the problem for a long time. This may be a symptom of not having fully articulated the costs and consequences of delay — go back and collect those in Step 4.

Maintain situational awareness because the ambiguous words may also be a sign you're talking to the Logical Customer (who is isolated from the costs and consequences of delay). Be prepared to bring the cost of delay into the conversation with questions that help overcome isolation: *"Who absorbs the costs while you are waiting?"* (Of course, put some padding in front of it so you don't sound abrasive; always follow the Recognize + Respond formula!)

Once you've gotten clarity around the exact date they want to begin the benefits of the solution, work backward with your prospect to realistically lay out a hypothetical calendar; this ends the myth that delay is free:

> *"In order for that to happen, we would need to [milestones, working back to the present] … . Is there anything that would prevent us from following that schedule?"*

Please note one small point of nuance: In this question, we ask, *"Is there anything that would prevent us from …"* This is an intentional choice! We want the prospect to think of all the reasons we couldn't do what we're asking. It's too easy to ask the simpler version of this question, which is, "Could we follow that schedule?" This won't prompt deep enough thought to smoke out anything that might, in fact, prevent us from following that schedule. It's a small point of nuance, but it matters.

When you lay out the milestones that need to be met in order for your prospect to have their pain fixed and the benefits flowing to them by their target date, you put into stark relief the reality that delay is not free.

This isn't false urgency — it's honesty. There are no free moves. You do not want your prospect to hold on to the costs and consequences of a problem you can solve just because some Logical Customer wants to wander through the weeds and think it over for the next nine quarters.

In this step, you're uncovering the real urgency of their pain. This isn't about you and your solution — it's about how much longer the prospect can live with the pains they've admitted to having. If they can hold on to those pains for another year, then you need to know before you ever go to the time and expense of putting an offer on the table.

IF THEY WANT IT NOW

Your prospect may answer, "I needed this fixed yesterday!" Don't get excited and prepare a proposal. This might be a Logical Customer whose false urgency gets salespeople to give them valuable information and quotes (Step 2 at Wimp Junction). Or it might be an Emotional Customer who genuinely wants their problem fixed, but they don't care about how it gets fixed; don't pitch how you'll fix it, or they'll send you down to the Logical Customer (where you'll end up at Wimp Junction).

Instead, simply funnel their answers down to further clarity so you understand what happens next:

> *"Yesterday? I'm afraid we haven't mastered time travel yet, and if you locked us in today, you'd start seeing the [benefits] start to show up on your dashboard in six months. So today is already October 5th. How much further beyond that do you think the enterprise wants to go?"*

This clarity-seeking question is a litmus test — you're testing their real urgency. You're testing whether this really is a problem worth fixing "yesterday." Logical Customers get slippery here: "Well, we'll need to gather some more data, and pull together our committee, and look at our options in the marketplace ..."

See how it's suddenly not urgent enough to have fixed in six months? That's why we don't believe them when they say they needed this fixed "yesterday."

If the Emotional Customer is telling you the truth, they'll answer honestly: "We can't go beyond October 5th." Do not start talking about implementation; they don't care about those details, and you'll only slow down your own sale. Instead, test their commitment with a slightly humorous question: *"Got your credit card?"* or *"Got a pen?"*

Now, you're getting into their evaluation and decision-making process. We'll talk more about that in the next chapter as we continue the Call Flow process with Step 7.

THE (NEXT) WORST QUESTION

At this point, we see a lot of rookie salespeople grasp the big picture but miss the nuance by changing this question about the prospect's timeline to, "When do you plan to make a decision?"

Never ask a prospect when they're going to make a decision! The prospects have dealt with enough amateur salespeople to know that the salesperson is really asking, "When do I get paid?" It destroys trust and rapport.

"When do you plan to make a decision?" is also too abstract and intellectual; it has nothing to do with alleviating pain. They may "make a decision" to think really hard about maybe pulling together a team to hire a consultant to assemble a committee to evaluate the options in the marketplace. None of that is even remotely related to alleviating their pain.

You need clarity around their pain calendar. What you're seeking to understand is exactly how much longer they can live with this pain.

So instead of asking when they'll make a decision, ask when are they hoping to have the pain resolved and benefits flowing: the ultimate goal of this entire process. For example, if your DV can help them get a new product to market faster, don't ask about when they plan to make a decision, sign a contract, or install your solution; instead, ask about *when they want to see their new product on shelves and new revenue flowing*. It might sound like this as you funnel their answers to clarity:

> *"When were you hoping to see the revenues from this new product line showing up on your dashboard?"*
> "By first quarter, for sure."
>
> *"Sounds reasonable. It helps if I understand what 'first quarter' means in this case since two people can say the same thing and be eighty-nine days apart. When within first quarter are you hoping to see the new revenues coming in?"*
> "We promised the Board by the end of Quarter 1, so March 31st."

> *"Makes sense. In the thousands of installations we've done with clients, we've found installation usually takes two weeks, the custom build takes about ninety days, and putting the specs together takes another ninety days, so you'd want to start putting the specs together by mid-October. Today is October 1st. Is there anything that would prevent us from following that schedule?"*

This clarity puts the cost of delay for each day they wait into sharp focus. If they can live with the pain a while longer, then perhaps you're there too early. Wait until it hurts enough to make a change. (Or perhaps the pain is there, but isolation is keeping them from connecting the dots. Go back and run the drill-down with them in Step 4 so they can articulate their pain!)

We just covered the first six steps in the Call Flow process to collect the Attributes of a Qualified Selling Opportunity and help your prospect become increasingly aware of the costs and consequences they're currently living with because they're not your customer.

Before we move on to the last three steps of the Call Flow process, I want to take some time to talk about handling pushbacks on your calls and maintaining situational awareness.

Handling Stalls

Your prospects will attempt to push back and stall your sale. They have responses to slow you down and move you onto the tracks of their buying system. These stalls can come from anyone in the cast of characters, though you're most likely to hear them from the Logical Customers.

Luckily, in our experience with more than 2,400 companies in over 170 industries, we can confidently tell you that all stalls generally fit into six broad categories.

We always ask salespeople in our training to give us every stall they hear in the marketplace. We start writing them onto a whiteboard, one by one. After we've listed the top four to six stalls, something delightful happens: Every new stall they add to the list ends up being a variation of one that's already on the board.

It's an incredibly eye-opening and liberating exercise. Sellers don't need to prepare to handle infinite different stalls. They simply need to have a strategy for the most common stalls; this will prepare them to handle just about any conversation they'll ever have in the marketplace, turning each stall into an opportunity to leverage their DV instead. Across every industry, here are the six most common stalls we find:

1. Madly in love: "I love my current vendor."
2. Just missed: "We just made a change" or "We just signed a ten-year agreement with your arch-competitor."
3. Bad history: "Your company gave us a bad experience that one time, and you'll never get our business again."
4. No issues: "I don't need what you're selling." (A variation might be, "I'm too busy for what you're selling.")
5. Checking out: "I'm retiring soon and don't want to rock the boat." (A variation might be, "I'm new here and don't want to rock the boat.")
6. Luau Invitation: "We're about to release an RFP; would you like to come?"

Stepping back another level, there's effectively one objection at the root of every stall: "I think I'm doing fine without you, and there are no consequences to me to block you from getting in here."

After articulating your DV in Chapter 4, you know there are, in fact, consequences to your prospect for not doing business with you. You can use those consequences to turn a stall into a conversation around your DV.

So, let's address the most common stalls you hear in your business and leverage your DV in your responses. You're a skilled seller, so you probably already have a bank of responses you use when prospects push back.

Here, I will ask you to rewrite them according to the Communication Keys we covered in Chapter 6 and weave your DV into them.

Grab a pencil and paper and make a list of the top four to six stalls you hear most often when selling to prospects:

1. _____

2. _____

3. _____

4. _____

5. _____

6. _____

Then, write out the responses you've typically been using for each stall:

1. _____

2. _____

3. _____

4. _____

5. _____

6. _____

Now, let's alter those responses using the principle of Recognize + Respond instead. Remember that, to keep your prospect in the OK chair, you never want to respond to stalls with a flat statement — it sounds too defensive, and suddenly you're debating with the prospect rather than cooperating with them. Simply acknowledge your prospect's stall and then gently respond with an Open-Ended Question that leverages your DV instead.

Remember, there are no free moves: If you have DV in this opportunity and your prospect successfully pushes you away, they will incur costs and consequences by missing out on your DV. Think about what those consequences might be and insert them into these questions.

1. Stall #1 Recognize + Respond with a DV Question:

_____

_____

2. Stall #2 Recognize + Respond with a DV Question:

_____

_____

3. Stall #3 Recognize + Respond with a DV Question:

_____

_____

4. Stall #4 Recognize + Respond with a DV Question:

_____

_____

5. Stall #5 Recognize + Respond with a DV Question:

_____

_____

6. Stall #6 Recognize + Respond with a DV Question:

_____

_____

The result of your work should be a bank of questions that cover the most common stalls you hear in the marketplace. Practice them until you're comfortable and congruent using them. Make sure you can deliver them smoothly from the Not OK chair so it doesn't turn into a confrontation with your prospect.

Here are some examples of ways you might respond to the most common stalls:

1. Madly in love: "I love my current vendor."
   "I'm sure they appreciate your business. What do you like most about what they do for you?"

   Listen quietly while they list everything they like! Let them get it all out onto the table. They want to validate their vendor selection and tell you everything they love. Let them. Do NOT go to solution by saying, "We do that, too!" Let them vent happily.

   "Mm-hmm. And what else do you like about their service?"
   "Mm-hmm. And what else do you like?"
   "Mm-hmm. And what else do you like?"
   "Mm-hmm. And what do you wish they did different or better?"

   NOW they'll tell you what gaps may exist. Now you know what

pain gaps YOU may be able to fill. But you'll never get this information unless you've first earned their engagement by listening patiently to everything they love and NOT jumping to self-defense.

2. Just missed: "We just made a change and signed a ten-year agreement with your arch-competitor."
   "Sounds like I'm here too late, and that's my fault. When a competitor comes and brings you an attractive option that isn't covered by your ten-year agreement and has value for you, how would you handle that?"

Remember, there are no free moves! If you have DV, then they're missing out on something you can provide (but your competitor can't). This question keeps the conversation going so you can explore those consequences.

3. Bad history: "Your company gave us a bad experience that one time, and you'll never get our business again."
   "Sounds like we didn't handle that very well. If you were us and wanted to try earning back your trust, what would that look like?"

Bad history is a difficult stall to overcome. We see it a lot in agriculture lending, where the family remembers that one time back in 1857 when the bank collected great-grandpa's farm and the family vowed to never work with them again.

It doesn't matter if you weren't around when the bad history happened. And you definitely don't want to jump to defending your company here because you'll only end up fighting with your prospect, and that's a fight you won't win. Simply stay in the Not OK chair and ask them humbly what it might take to try earning back their trust. Their answers may surprise you and gain you further engagement.

4. No issues: "I don't need what you're selling."
   "Sounds like paradise! May I ask a question before I go? How many serious competitors do you have in your business?" ... "And how satisfied are you with the market share you're currently getting?

Put your hand on the doorknob! Human nature wants what it can't have, and being willing to walk away may prompt an honest conversation with your prospect. They've never had a seller leave them alone. If you ask this question from the Not OK chair, and in the context of your exit, you'll likely extend the conversation.

Also, please note the nuanced language around "how satisfied are you." This is an effective way to open a gap in the prospect's mind that things could be different or better. The word "satisfied" is an emotive word that resonates more deeply than intellectual words like "think" or "do." It's an innocent question that extends the conversation. (You will be tempted to ask its closed-ended cousin, "Are you satisfied with ..." Don't ask that — it's a trap close between yes and no, and your prospect will feel like you're setting them up to say, "Well, gosh, no, I'm not satisfied!" Stick with the open-ended version, and you'll keep your prospect's rapport.)

5. Checking out: "I'm retiring soon and don't want to rock the boat." (A variation might be, "I'm new here and don't want to rock the boat.")

   "Sounds like I'm here too late for you, and too early for the next person ... . When you explained to the Board that you weren't taking on projects and wanted to make sure they were comfortable taking on the hundred-million-dollar loss you could have fixed, what was their reaction?"

   Remember, there are no free moves! This is probably a Logical Customer who is reasonably covering their own position in the enterprise. Unfortunately, their decision to defer a solution costs the enterprise something, and they're isolated from those consequences. Bring the cost of delay into your conversation with the Logical Customer, but do it in a way that assumes they had the professional courtesy to inform the Emotional Customer that they'd have to live with the problem longer.

6. Luau invitation: "We're about to release an RFP; would you like to come?"

   "I'm not sure ... . What are the most important things you're hoping the RFP will do for you?"

   This gives you an opportunity to uncover critically important information: What's most important to them in their evaluation and decision-making process?

   Most RFP processes are run by Logical Customers whose primary focus is lowest price. Everything looks like a commodity on their spreadsheet. But they'll answer you here with vague language like "great value," "speed," and "service." Let them answer, and then ask for more:

"Mm-hmm. What else will be important to you in your selection of a solution provider?"
"Mm-hmm. What else?"

Get it all out on the table, then ask the most important question of all:
"I notice you didn't say anything about [solving the problem only your DV can solve]. What should we assume about that?"

Get ahead of their RFP process and help them value your DV in their selection criteria above lowest price. Then you can win.

Throughout the Sale

As you move through these steps, you must remember No-Fail Selling Rule #8: Always know where you are in YOUR process.

NO-FAIL RULE #8
Always know where you are in *your* process.

Military commanders call this "situational awareness." You cannot be blinded by your sale's apparent progress and forget where you are on the proverbial train tracks. Check your surroundings. You must know what happened on every call.

Before your sales call, take some time to honestly assess where you are in your process of collecting the Attributes of a Qualified Selling Opportunity and what you want to accomplish on the next call. Do you already have Steps 1-3 done, and now you need to proceed through Steps 4 and beyond? Plan your Call Flow.

Also plan for the stalls you're most likely to hear from the prospect on your next call if they push back, and prepare some responses using the techniques we've taught you here.

And after every call, do a quick assessment to make sure that what you think happened on your call actually happened. Were you talking to the right person? Do you have clarity? Enough to move forward? This regular honest assessment will keep you on your tracks.

Quick diagnostic check

Let me give you two common features that indicate the salesperson "wimped out" somewhere in these first six steps (but doesn't realize it yet). If you have either of these features, your sale is probably dead:

1. You're still being called a vendor: This probably means you haven't differentiated yourself from the competition, and you're on track for an RFP/RFQ bidding war.
2. You're still trapped at the Logical Customer, and you're being blocked from knowing what will be most important to the Emotional Customers: This means you're being commoditized.

Three Questions to Stay on Track

As your sale progresses, I want you to keep in mind and regularly answer three questions about the level of commitment between you and your prospect:

1. Do you match the prospect's commitment?
2. Are you constantly evaluating your investment?
3. Are you confirming commitment regularly?

Do not skip this assessment. Do not move forward without verifying these three things:

1. You Have Commitment Rapport

Never get ahead of your prospect's level of commitment to doing business with you.

Throughout most of the sales process, the prospect is sure to be quite comfortable with the concept of never becoming your customer. If you are uncomfortable with that concept and they are comfortable with it, you will be out of rapport, and sales are difficult in those circumstances.

You must be as comfortable as they are with the idea of them never being your customer, and your language must gently communicate that there is a match (rapport) between their thinking on this point and yours. (Match their commitment, but don't exceed it, or you'll remind them of the last grasping salesperson who crossed their path.)

As you move through the sales process, you will be indicating your awareness that they have the option of not doing business with you. It will be done with soft comments, indicating this may be the wrong time to start the process, or there may not be a fit between what they would look for and what you do well, or that your solutions could be overkill for the problem they want to solve.

Because you have very specific goals, and not everyone is a prospect, it is essential that you get comfortable with ending it when it is confirmed that this is not going to culminate in a sale for you. If they get the idea that you want to do business with them more than they want to do business with you, that is a Wimp Junction point where your margins go up in smoke.

2. You're Thinking Like a Business Person

One of the challenges business people face is the intelligent investment of limited resources. In your case, those resources include your time, your knowledge, and the expertise and resources your organization brings to the pursuit of a complex sale.

Since complex sales are expensive to conduct and your resources are finite, you must constantly assess the quality of the opportunity you are pursuing and ask, "Is this one I can win at an acceptable level of investment of my resources?" As soon as you do not like the answer, you need to move on.

Of course, it will come as no shock to recognize that your prospects are constantly running their version of the same assessment. However, because you bring useful information and competitive leverage to the prospects, they may want to keep you engaged longer than it is in your interest to stay involved. Throughout the process, you must continue to collect the Attributes of a Qualified Selling Opportunity, and when those Attributes do not meet your requirements, you have a business decision to make.

You must be comfortable walking away when the investment of your time and resources no longer makes sense. Interestingly, when you're openly discussing that it may be time for you to move on, you may encounter a peculiar phenomenon of human behavior: Humans crave what they can't have. As you put your hand on the door handle to leave, your prospect may quickly indicate that they do not, in fact, want you to leave. This tends to help your case.

3. You've Confirmed Commitment at Each Stage

At every step in your sale, you must ensure that the buyer is as committed as you, the seller, because you have expensive resources that will be deployed as you get deeper into the process. It is irresponsible to disregard the signals of unequal commitment.

As you progress through the stages of your sale, you must periodically reconfirm that both parties are equally committed. To what they are committed will adjust as they get deeper into the process. For example, in the beginning, there must be mutual commitment to an honest exploration of the fit between your ideal customer, their ideal solution, and the recognition of any gaps on either side.

Later in the process, there must be mutual commitment to fully evaluating costs of their problems or of not being your customer, as well as their expected spend, when they wanted the solution in place, their process to select a solution provider, and what they will do if you come back with a solution that fits.

This constant communication is outside the comfort zone of many salespeople, who only want to talk about their solution. But to close a complex sale, you must maintain clarity and situational awareness through the entire length of the Last Mile. You'll never close an already-dead deal by avoiding clarity.

Disqualifying

When we teach salespeople about collecting the Attributes of a Qualified Selling Opportunity, we are often asked, "Is it possible to accidentally disqualify a good opportunity?" Salespeople get nervous that they may lose a viable opportunity through overzealous qualification.

Our answer is that it's practically impossible to accidentally disqualify a good opportunity if you're following the stages on the right side of the tracks at Wimp Junction.

For a quick recap, those stages so far are:

- *Differentiate* yourself by determining your DV in this opportunity.
- Use your DV to *Target* the right Emotional Customers.
- *Engage* those Emotional Customers with strategic questions that bring clarity to the costs and consequences they're experiencing in the absence of your DV.

When this flow is followed with focus and clarity, you're more likely to uncover hitherto-buried pains than you are to disqualify a good opportunity. In other words, you're more likely to uncover new opportunities than you are to accidentally discard a winnable deal.

Occasionally, we do see an eager salesperson skip the effort to strategically Differentiate and Target, and go straight to engaging a Logical Customer. When the Logical Customer lies to them by saying, "We don't need what you're selling," the salesperson takes it at face value and moves to the next prospect on their list without digging any deeper. They think they're following a good process to qualify. There might be a missed opportunity here, but it certainly wasn't missed through the ruthless pursuit of clarity.

If you follow the steps to pursue clarity as we're outlining here, it's practically impossible to discard a viable opportunity. You're more likely to unearth previously missed opportunities than to accidentally disqualify a good one. Go forth with confidence, follow the steps, and qualify ruthlessly.

Cooling Off?

As you move through the final stages of your selling system, you may encounter new reluctance from the prospect to match your commitment to the process.

You must recognize it for what it is and verify your perceptions. If you are sensing that your commitment may be greater than theirs, it is time to indicate that you may have to walk. You don't ever want to be more committed to fixing their problem than they are, or you'll get ahead of the prospect, which leads to a Think It Over and the loss of a sales opportunity.

Of course, the expression of your willingness to walk is critical. You must make sure as you discuss the possibility this isn't a fit that you do not state anything negative about the prospect, their organization, their process, or your competition.

How do you do that? Take a lesson from the psychology of maintaining healthy relationships. We have a friend who is an expert in building and maintaining healthy interpersonal relationships, and one of the golden principles he teaches is that in a two-party discussion, one party may have to assume more than half the fault in order for the other person to be willing to stay engaged now or in the future. The key phrase is some form of *"It's my fault."*

In your sale, when you need to open the topic of ending it and walking, it will help if you are willing to make any barriers, problems, or lack of understanding your fault.

It may sound like this:

> *"Over the years of helping customers solve problems like we have been discussing, I have learned that it doesn't work for me to get ahead of the customer with regard to the degree of commitment to solving the problem. It's probably my fault that I did not recognize that this may not be the right time for us to pursue this solution. What do you think?"*

CHAPTER EIGHT

Commit

The Prospect's Buying System

Your System

STEP 1

The prospect lies
to the salesperson.

STEP 2

The prospect gets the
salesperson to provide
valuable information
and a quote.

STEP 3

The prospect lies
about what's going
to happen next.

STEP 4

The prospect doesn't
answer or return the
salesperson's calls.

STAGE 1
Differentiate

STAGE 2
Target

STAGE 3
Engage

STAGE 4
Commit

STAGE 5
Secure

STRATEGIC

We're close to presenting an offer to do business with our prospect. It's tempting to get excited at this stage because we've made it this far, but we cannot lose our situational awareness. We're still collecting the Attributes of a Qualified Selling Opportunity (QSO).

We must maintain a steady cadence, especially at this high-risk stage. Ninety percent of all preventable losses happen here at the Commit stage because the salesperson "wimps out" by getting impatient and not going deep enough.

In this Commit stage, there are only three steps to finish our Call Flow. In these steps, we are looking for validation of your prospect's process, authority, and intention. We're seeking total clarity and avoiding Unpaid Consulting. These steps move us beyond merely Engaging the prospect to Committing with them to finish the process.

If the prospect has lied to you along the way about their process, authority, or intention, you will find the lie at this stage — but only if you funnel your conversations correctly.

Here are the last three steps in your Call Flow. You don't need to plan a separate conversation for them; you can just continue smoothly on the heels of Step 6 if your sale is on a roll. (In fact, if you're talking to the right person and find actionable pain, these steps needn't happen any later than your second conversation.)

CONFIRM EVAL   AGREE   AGREE
& DECISION   ON CLEAR   TO MOVE
PROCESS   OUTCOMES   FORWARD

The order of these final three steps is intentional because it completely kills Think It Overs. Doing these final three steps in this order gets the fiction out of your forecast. If your prospect has lied about their intent or authority, it tends to show up here. If you're having trouble getting clear answers here, it means you may be too low in the organization.

Our goal in this stage is to get a decision: either "Yes" or "No." A yes-or-no answer means you have a clean forecast. A Think It Over means you have no clear next step, and there's fiction in your forecast. If the answer is Yes, you'll get the business and the money. If the answer is No, you'll get the lesson from it, get better, and get the business and the money next time.

TACTICAL: Call Flow 7–9

Call Flow 7: *Confirm that the evaluation and decision-making processes are understood*

You cannot win a game if you do not understand how to play it. You must attain clarity around how your prospect evaluates solutions like yours and then makes their final decision to do or not do business with you. Ninety percent of all preventable losses happen here!

It can start with a simple question:

> *"Organizations vary greatly as to their processes to evaluate a solution proposal if one were offered. Please help me understand the evaluation and decision-making process you use to decide whether or not to accept a solution proposal if one were offered."*

This question efficiently accomplishes two things:

1. The quick story at the front (*"Organizations vary greatly ..."*) indicates your wider industry knowledge and experience. This shows your prospect that you've solved this problem more often than they have; your experiential *n* is higher than theirs. This builds your credibility.

2. The conditional tense (*" ... if a solution were offered"*) leaves open the possibility that a solution may not be offered. *This is how you stay in commitment rapport with the prospect and avoid wimping out.* You don't yet know if you have a Qualified Selling Opportunity, so you can't guarantee you'll present anything. This reminds the prospect of your willingness to walk, which tends to strengthen your position later if they try to squeeze you on price.

Once you've asked about their evaluation and decision-making process, drill down and clarify the ambiguous words. Expect to have at least five or six exchanges back and forth to clarify their ambiguous words. Remember, nine out of ten preventable losses happen because the salesperson didn't go deep enough here.

A simple question to remember while you're funneling is, *"And then what?"* I'm not recommending you literally ask the question of your prospect — it's too abrasive and needs some padding. But it's the question you must be able to answer, again and again, so you know what really happens in their process to evaluate and decide on a solution provider. Let's use a simple example to illustrate. A salesperson asks our above question:

> *"Please help me understand the evaluation and decision-making process you use to decide whether or not to accept a solution proposal if one were offered."*

The prospect may answer like this:

"Well, I'm the final decision maker." (They probably aren't! Funnel down for clarity with a simple Recognize + Respond to find out what happens next.)

"It's nice to be talking to the right person. Just so I understand, what's the rest of your process once you've made your decision?"

"I'll let my team know I've given the green light."

"Great, that'll make things easy. After you've given the green light, what happens next?"

"We'll do our site visits, etc."

"Sounds good. And if that all goes well, what could we expect to happen next?"

"Well, then it'll go to the Board at that point."

"Makes sense. Boards are usually full of astute business people who ask great questions. What questions should we anticipate getting from them?"

"Well, that depends on what we find in our site visits, etc."

"Mm-hmm. You're an experienced professional, and you've clearly done this before. What tends to be most important to the Board when they're evaluating your recommendation?"

"Definitely the overall value of the solution."

"Sounds reasonable. But 'value' is one of those words that means different things to different people; please help me understand what value means in this context."

> "They'll want to make sure we don't pay too much for a solution, if we can get the same thing at a lower price."

Now you're getting into the depths of their evaluation and decision-making process! You're getting clarity around where in the process you may get points for your DV, and where you might be commoditized.

In this case, the prospect enterprise doesn't yet seem to have a way to reconcile price and TCOOL. Even if the Board intuitively wants the highest-quality, lowest-overall-cost solution, they'll be looking at all the solutions next to each other on a spreadsheet helpfully assembled by the Logical Customer; all the solutions look alike on the spreadsheet, and this decision will probably ultimately go to lowest price. That's a game you can't win — unless you alter the decision-making process to favor your DV over someone else's lowest price:

> *"Sure. And if it turns out that the lowest-priced solution ends up being the one with the highest total business costs, how will they resolve that?"*

YOUR GOAL

At this step, you're looking for clarity around their process to evaluate and decide whether or not to do business with you.

In the almost four decades we've been coaching enterprises and salespeople through complex sales, this is the step where salespeople are most likely to get stuck at Wimp Junction. They may have effectively traversed the first few stages on the right side of the tracks, but their momentum leads them to optimistically and prematurely conclude that this deal is closer to signing than it really is — and they fail to dig deep enough here.

Even experienced sellers can find themselves surprised at this step. We recently worked with an elite seller — we'll call her Maria — who had expertly figured out her DV for the opportunity, targeted her Emotional Customers with laser focus, avoided Logical Customers, and guided the sale through the entire Call Flow process to collect the Attributes of a Qualified Selling Opportunity.

She presented an offer to do business to her highest-ranking Emotional Customer. However, because she had done this many times before with great success, she'd gotten a little too comfortable in this sale and had failed to ask all the questions she needed to ask around this particular prospect's decision-making process.

It turned out that her highest-ranking Emotional Customer could green-light the offer, but then — as in many large bureaucratic organizations — that contract would have to be processed through and given the final stamp of approval by ... Procurement.

Maria hadn't realized this and wasn't expecting the email she received a few days later from a Logical Customer in Procurement, explaining that Maria would have to take a 20% cut or there'd be no deal.

These unexpected turns are normal in complex sales, where complicated organizations have complicated processes in place for making changes — usually designed to protect against making changes.

Luckily, Maria had developed a strong case for the cost of delay with her Emotional Customer. One strategic phone call reminding them of that cost of delay (especially compared to the smaller 20% cut the Logical Customer was demanding) helped convince them to, with some effort, get around the roadblocks and finally close the deal.

To avoid those last-minute surprises, which can often derail a solid opportunity, this seventh step will help you thoroughly understand your prospect's process:

- What is their process to evaluate solutions like this?
- What is their process to decide on a solution like this?
- What's most important to each person who's voting?
- How will they resolve their differences when they don't agree?
- Where will you get points for your Differentiating Value (DV) in this process?
- What is the relationship between DV and price?
- Who are the third parties — the other decision-makers, stakeholders, and snipers?
- What are their agendas?
- What will the "Meeting After the Meeting" look like?

When there are multiple stakeholders with competing interests, you need to know how this enterprise will resolve those differences and what will be most important to each person who votes. This clarity will help you foresee risks like unanticipated third parties in the cast of characters and what really happens in the "Meeting After the Meeting."

THIRD-PARTY AGENDAS

Chances are, the prospect you're talking to isn't the final decision-maker, even if they think they are. Most purchase decisions need to be run past third parties like budget committees, business partners, Boards of Directors, spouses, consultants, bank covenants, the old guy who lives on a boat in Florida who put up the money ... there's usually someone else who has a say in this deal. You need to understand what's on their agendas.

When you've unearthed a third party, pull their agenda into this conversation by asking: *"What questions should we anticipate from [the banker, the Board, the spouse] so that you have all the answers?"*

Your goal is to attain clarity about what's important to them and about their role in the process. You don't want any surprises later!

MEETING AFTER THE MEETING

The "Meeting After the Meeting" (MAM) is a term we use at Slattery to refer to the meeting held by various stakeholders at your prospect organization to discuss your offer to do business after you've presented it and have departed.

The MAM may be an actual meeting on your prospects' calendars or simply the process by which these stakeholders ultimately decide what to do with your offer. In any case, they will convene somehow to discuss and settle their differences about your proposal after you're gone.

Imagine a long conference table in a board room at your prospect organization, with all the various stakeholders sitting around it for the MAM, and a tiny little microphone hanging from the ceiling so you can listen to their discussion after you've presented your solution and left the building. If you could eavesdrop, what would you hear? Who sitting around the table gets to vote on this? What's most important to each of them? And, most importantly, how will the enterprise reconcile the different priorities?

These are the questions you should be able to answer so you can pull the MAM into your conversations across the cast of characters.

If you find one stakeholder will defend the incumbent against you because they want to avoid the pain of change, then you can strategically ask questions around the cost of keeping the problem while the incumbent tries again to fix it and fails. If you find the Logical Customer will do whatever it takes to go with the lowest price, you can ask how they plan to reconcile the difference between up-front price and total cost to the enterprise. The MAM will still happen without you, but you will have influenced it in your favor and mitigated any unexpected surprises.

THE ONLY THREE ANSWERS

When you ask a question, there are only three types of possible responses you'll get from a prospect: positive, negative, or inquiry. These responses indicate their willingness to cooperate and move forward.

Here's what those three responses might sound like when you're asking your prospect questions about their evaluation and decision-making process:

Positive Response: The prospect is cooperating with you.
- "We have this committee ..."
- "We've identified you and two other contenders ..."
- "Site visits, demo ..."

If you get these affirmative answers, listen carefully, funnel down to clarity, and take notes — they're giving you valuable information. Keep your ears open for any third parties, like a Board of Directors, who get to have a say in your sale.

Negative Response: The prospect is stalling you.

◆ "We won't reveal our process."

◆ "That's not something we share with vendors."

"Vendor"? Red flag! If you're still getting called a vendor, you're column fodder. Your sale is probably dead, but if you want to give it another shot, go back to Steps 1–6 and finish collecting the Attributes of a QSO.

Inquiry Response: The prospect wants to know more.

◆ "Why do you need to know that?"

Tread carefully here because you may have lost (or not yet earned) their trust and rapport. Maybe you tried to jump out of the Not OK chair a few times. Or perhaps they're just genuinely curious. Either way, you can be open about the investment of your effort, time, and resources to putting together a solution. Stay soft, tell the truth, and keep them in the OK chair.

> *"Our management asks that we have clarity about what happens next after we design a solution and what your process is to evaluate that effort, since it involves a considerable investment of time and resources. Would there be any reason we couldn't understand that now?"*

Please note the nuance here: We don't ask, "Could we understand ..." but rather, we want to ask, *"Would there be any reason we couldn't?"* It's a much softer and more effective question.

CAST OF CHARACTERS

Here's a useful exercise that will help bring clarity at this stage. Take an organizational chart like the one below and fill it out with the cast of characters at your prospect organization related to your sale. Don't leave anyone off.

Beside each contact, indicate:

◆ DP = they participate in decision-making process
◆ LDP = leader of decision-making process
◆ EC = Emotional Customer
◆ LC = Logical Customer
◆ COP = Consequences of Pain (they get the bill for not having your DV)
◆ P = this contact's most important pain is validated

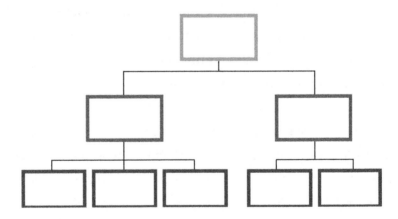

Complex sales tend to have a full cast of characters. Make sure you know the full cast of characters you're dealing with here. The Emotional Customers, the Logical Customers, that one guy in Purchasing who would rather sink the ship than move the business away from the incumbent supplier ... fill this out completely.

Many of our clients have found that, by simply sketching out an org chart like this, they get a clearer strategic view of the opportunity as it approaches the final stage of the sales process. They're especially able to spot threats that they otherwise would have missed in these critical last steps. Even if you know the players well, sketch the cast of characters onto an org chart like this, and you may find yourself spotting imminent threats or opportunities to accelerate your sale toward closure.

DRIVE YOUR DV INTO THEIR PROCESS

As you learn about this prospect's evaluation and decision-making process, you will have a chance to drive your DV into their process so that your unique differentiators become more valuable than another competitor's low price (or other concessions). Here's what it might sound like. Let's say you ask the question:

> *"It varies from one enterprise to another as to what things are important when deciding whether or not to change solution providers. Please help me understand: What factors will be most important to you [or the board, or any other third parties] in your analysis?"*

Clarify their answers — you'll probably hear "value," "quality," "reliability," etc. — and then ask some version of: *"Mm-hmm. And what else will be important to you [or the Board, or any other third parties]?"* Then ask again: *"Mm-hmm. And what else?"* And ask again: *"Mm-hmm. And what else?"*

When you've allowed them to exhaust their list of priorities, then you can drive your DV into the conversation:

"I notice you didn't say anything about [solving the problem only your DV can solve]. What should we assume about that?"

"I notice you didn't mention needing control over all business costs; what should we assume about that?"

"I notice you didn't mention anything about time to market; what should we assume about that?"

"I notice you didn't mention anything about controlling your own data; what should we assume about that?"

If they haven't thought about it (and they probably haven't), your DV is at risk of being undervalued in their evaluation and decision-making process. Your simple question here will help bring an awareness that there are no free moves and that missing out on your DV will have real consequences.

Whatever their answer may be, funnel it down to clarity — remember, you may need five or six exchanges here to get to clarity! For example, let's say you ask: *"I notice you didn't mention needing control over all business costs; what should we assume about that?"*

They answer: "I'm not sure we need to worry about that."
"Mm-hmm. Tell me more."

"Well, we've been pretty good about controlling our business costs and optimizing efficiencies, so we're not really worried there."
"Makes sense. How big would it have to be to warrant some concern?"

"Ten percent."

"That's not too bad. If that were available to you now, when would you want to know?"

DISRUPTION

Once you thoroughly understand your prospect's evaluation and decision-making process, be prepared to disrupt it with your willingness to walk away.

Maybe your prospect tells you: "We'll start with twelve potential vendors, narrow it down with an RFP, then stage a fight to the death between two finalists." Maybe you find out that you'll have to sell to committees. Maybe your prospect will demand impossible contract terms. Maybe they'll perform marginectomies until enough contenders walk and there's just one left.

To survive such threats with your margins intact, you must always be prepared to walk away. You indicate this clearly but gently, like using the word "if" instead of "when": *"Help us understand how you would evaluate a solution if one were offered."*

You'll only present if it's in the interest of both parties, and fueling a bidding war isn't in your best interest. Always stay in the Not OK chair when you indicate your willingness to walk: *"It sounds like this might not be the right time for us; that's my fault. What do you think?"*

If you truly have Differentiating Value, and you've communicated that DV to the right people, then *they want you in the race.* Your willingness to walk keeps you from being commoditized. They'll only be able to squeeze you if you're too desperate for the sale to walk away from it. Don't wimp out here. Don't settle for letting your margins get wiped out by low prices or contract terms from hell. You must sell on value; stick to it here. Be willing to walk if your DV isn't valued.

Call Flow Step 8: *Agree on clear outcomes*

In Call Flow 7, you confirmed that your prospect can make a decision. Here in Call Flow 8, you confirm that they would, in fact, make a decision if a proposal were offered. This hypothetical question keeps you from doing proposals and presentations for people who can't or won't act on them. Here's what it sounds like:

> *"I want to make sure I understand: If we design the enhancements that you said would address these problems you're having, and the design reflects your goals, and as we discussed we're going to charge you approximately $X to do it, and we answer all of your questions ... what would you do next?"*

You are looking for the prospect's commitment to follow their own process, which they just described to you in Call Flow 7. This ensures they didn't lie about their authority or intentions. Commitment means they will either take action and accept your offer to do business — or the discussion is done, and you're not going any further. You and the prospect must be comfortable with either outcome.

You're agreeing to pursue clear outcomes together. If they start waffling, if you pick up on cognitive dissonance, if what they're saying now doesn't match what they said earlier, then they may be lying to you. You may not actually have a qualified opportunity here.

You can gently probe for truth without calling them a liar: *"I think you just told me you wanted to keep the problem longer ... What am I missing?"* (This "What am I missing" question makes it your fault and keeps them in the OK chair.)

Your goal at this step is to determine:
1. Have they lied about their intent?
2. Have they lied about their authority?

If you try to proceed before you have clarity around those questions, you'll get a Think It Over at Wimp Junction.

When they answer you, be prepared to funnel their ambiguous answer to clarity. They may tell you, "We'll go forward." You need to have clarity around the phrase "go forward." Does that mean going to contract? Implementation? Pilot? Another demo? A committee to think it over for the next twenty-seven months? Ask another question, and keep pursuing clarity: *"Going forward to us means [this]. Will that work for you?"*

Call Flow Step 9: *Attain mutual agreement to move forward*

In this final step, your goal is to attain a clear commitment from your prospect that they will actually follow their own process when you put an offer on the table. In the context of your hypothetical question at Call Flow 8 ("What would you do next?"), it's a reality check ("What will you do next?"). It may sound like this:

> *"Would there be any reason you couldn't give me a yes-or-no answer after we've reviewed our offer, answered your questions, and ensured no surprises?"*

While we normally recommend Open-Ended Questions like who, where, what, when, and how, this question is intentionally designed to be a binary yes-or-no question at the very bottom of the funnel to clarity, where space is tight and the pace is fast.

Your goal here is to find out:
1. Will they follow their process?
2. Will they make a timely decision?
3. Do they understand and want to minimize the costs and consequences of delay?

Agree that you will leave every presentation of an offer with a decision

The worst outcome when presenting an offer to do business is any version of Think It Over. You'll avoid it if you agree with your prospect that you'll leave your presentation with a decision. Giving them permission to tell you "No" is key to this agreement. They're not committing to buy your stuff here; they're committing to let you leave your presentation with either a yes or a no answer.

It sounds like this: *"At the end of the meeting/presentation, we'll ask you to make a decision: yes or no. If yes, you'll take it to your board to approve. If no, you won't — and that's fine. I'll take a no! Don't send me back to my office waiting for the phone to ring. Is there any reason we couldn't get a yes or no from you at the end of that meeting?"*

Even if they have to take it to a third party in a Meeting After the Meeting, you can request clarity around what they'll recommend: *"Is there any reason you couldn't tell me what your recommendation will be?"* or, *"You can tell me, 'I'll recommend you,' or, 'You're a distant second.' Either is fine!"*

Remember, the real purpose here is to get a complete under-standing of how this will go down. If they've withheld anything, you'll smoke it out here. If they've been open and honest, then their answer will sound like this: "Sure, we can give you a yes or no at the end of your presentation."

If they've withheld information, then their answer will sound like this: "No, we can't do that." You can reply gently with a Recognize + Respond: *"Sounds like I might have missed something about your process — that's my fault. Please help me understand what I've missed."* Their answer will probably give you a hint of what they withheld: "Well, we'll have to ..." There it is — the real process you're facing.

NO TRIAL CLOSES

Please note the nuance here: We're not doing a "trial close" wherein the salesperson asks, "If we do this, will you buy it?" That's a selling trick we avoid because it attempts to trap the prospect into committing to something they haven't yet had a chance to fully evaluate. Their consent and cooperation remain paramount through this process. We're not asking them to com-mit to buying.

Instead, we're effectively asking: *Will you follow your own pro-cess?* We don't need to know what the outcome will be — but we must know that there will be an outcome. This is how we avoid leaving presentations with Think It Overs.

In this stage, we're seeking clarity around whether they will make a decision. That's it. This is about their process, not our stuff. Do not ask them to commit to buying your stuff before you've pre-sented it. It puts your prospect in an impossibly awkward position, and it doesn't even secure any real commitment to making an honest decision.

Instead, finish your Call Flow steps and agree on clear outcomes together. If they aren't planning to make a decision in response to your offer, then you need to know that before putting an offer together at all.

THE PURPOSE OF THIS STEP

This step smokes out any lies they've given you along the way. It's potent.

If they've been honest with you, and the cost of the problem is on the table, and the cost of delay is clearly identified, and they've agreed that the problem must stop by a certain date, and they've been open with you about their evaluation and decision-making process, then they will have no trouble agreeing to follow their own process and move forward here.

But if they've lied about their intent, and they don't intend to make a change at all, this request for mutual commitment before moving forward will make them very squirrely! They want you to provide valuable information and a quote, but they don't want to commit to anything. This might be a Logical Customer who's been masquerading as the Emotional Customer; they have neither the authority nor the intent to commit, and this question will smoke it out.

There's also a chance that there have been changes at your prospect organization over the course of your sale (remember, complex sales can take months to conduct), and this final check for commitment helps smoke out any changes that might sabotage your sale. We've seen late-stage deals disrupted by unannounced mergers and acquisitions more than once.

This question will smoke out any final unforeseen reservations or obstacles your prospect may have that will keep them from committing to clear outcomes.

YOUR FAULT

As you seek your prospect's commitment to mutually-agreed-upon next steps in the final stages of your sale, you may encounter issues or resistance that indicate you need to walk away. If that occurs and you end your engagement, then you must indicate that its ending is your fault, not the prospect's. Even if they lied, you "misunderstood."

This isn't just humility for the sake of humility. If the issues are resolved and the deal can move forward again, you've strategically protected the relationship. (You'll never win a deal with an offended prospect, no matter how "right" you were when you called them out.)

And if the issues aren't resolved and the deal doesn't go forward, you've strategically protected your name and reputation during departure. Never underestimate the breadth of a prospect's connections or their potential to harm you in the marketplace. There's nothing to gain by debating or finger-pointing, but there's much to gain by being the adult and keeping your prospect in the OK chair.

If you end up walking away from the deal, that's okay — remember, you're going through these Call Flow steps in order to qualify your sales opportunity. Only fully Qualified Selling Opportunities are worth investing in; don't worry about walking away from deals that don't meet your standards because the chances of winning in unqualified deals are too low.

Simply make sure that when you do walk away from an unwinnable opportunity, you do so with humility and keep your prospect in the OK chair at all times.

You've completed the nine steps of your Call Flow sales process, taking you through the Engage and Commit stages of your sale. You know your prospect's decision-making process, and you know it'll work for you.

There's only one stage left in the sales process: Secure.

CHAPTER NINE

Secure

The Prospect's Buying System		Your System

STEP 1
The prospect lies to the salesperson.

STEP 2
The prospect gets the salesperson to provide valuable information and a quote.

STEP 3
The prospect lies about what's going to happen next.

STEP 4
The prospect doesn't answer or return the salesperson's calls.

STAGE 1
Differentiate

STAGE 2
Target

STAGE 3
Engage

STAGE 4
Commit

STAGE 5
Secure

STRATEGIC

You're almost ready to Secure your sale. *Almost.*

Attributes = Accurate Forecast

This moment is critical; too many salespeople rush ahead without checking their situational awareness, and their sale fails at the Secure stage. Just because someone is threatening to spend money in your part of the economy doesn't mean you have a real opportunity.

Go down this checklist to make sure your deal has all the Attributes of a Qualified Selling Opportunity. You'll recognize the Attributes — they are the steps you followed one by one in your Call Flow sales process.

But here, you're going to look back with 20/20 hindsight and honest clarity, and assess your deal through the lens of these qualifying Attributes.

If you do not have *every single box* checked by the end of this chapter, do *not* move forward into the Secure stage — your sale is not on solid enough footing.

Let's begin.

1. **You've gained agreement to the sales process.**
   Has the prospect agreed to engage with you in order to explore a solution that might have value for them? (And did you get this agreement from the highest-ranking Emotional Customers who will vote on this? Do a quick check to make sure Logical Customers weren't the only ones you were engaging with here.)
2. **You've collected pains from the prospect.**
   Did your prospect articulate the pains they're experiencing without your DV? You want to hear at least three enterprise pains so you're not selling a single-pain solution. (The only exception

to this is when they're experiencing one major existential pain, but those are rare.)

3. **You've confirmed the order of importance of pains and problems.**

   Do you know which pains and problems are the most important to each person who votes in this decision? (Not limited to only enterprise pains and problems — you want to know the unique priorities of each person involved in this decision-making process.)

4. **You've extracted all costs of pains and problems.**

   Did they articulate all the ways they're currently paying to keep each problem? Do they agree they are paying too much without you?

5. **You've confirmed adequate resources are available.**

   Have you discussed what they're expecting to spend to fix the problem and relieve the pain? (This has nothing to do with your solution!) Do you know how they arrived at that number? Will the funds be available?

6. **You've drawn out the exact date to begin harvesting the benefits of a solution.**

   Does the prospect have an exact date when they want to begin harvesting the benefits of the solution? (This has nothing to do with decisions or implementations!) Remember, "soon" doesn't count.

7. **You've confirmed their evaluation and decision-making processes.**

   Do you understand all aspects, participants, criteria, and timing of the prospect's process to evaluate and decide whether or not to do business with you? (This includes all third-party participants, such as bosses, owners, CPAs, advisors, and Boards.) Do you know what happens next at each step? Most importantly, do you understand exactly where and how you will get points for your DV?

8. You've agreed on clear outcomes.

Has your prospect agreed to make a yes-or-no decision if a proposal were offered? (Have they agreed not to Think It Over?) You want to know that they would follow the process they described.

9. You've attained mutual agreement to move forward.

Have you set clear agreements as to exactly what happens if you offer a solution? Have you agreed that you'll leave any presentation of an offer to do business with a decision?

If you have confirmed that you have all Nine Attributes of a fully Qualified Selling Opportunity, then let's move forward and Secure your sale.

TACTICAL

You've completed the first four stages of your selling system, and you've verified that you have all the Attributes of a Qualified Selling Opportunity.

Now you're ready to Secure the sale. You can present your solution and an offer to do business! (Please note: This presentation is not the same as a capabilities presentation, in which your prospect learns general information about the things your solution can do for them. A capabilities presentation might have already happened in early discussions or might even live on your website. This presentation, at the end of your sales process, is where you present an offer to do business, with valuable details and customized information for this prospect around your solution and its pricing.)

Since this is a complex sale, and you're not just responding to RFPs and RFQs (right?), you'll most likely present an offer to do business "live" to your prospect(s). This might amount to a phone call with your Emotional Customer; an in-person, multi-hour, stand-up speech with a live demonstration; or anything in between.

Whatever it looks like, your presentation is the moment you present your solution in its full glory, radiating with Differentiating Value. It's a favorite moment for many salespeople, but it does carry some risk. Stay alert.

Keep Moving Forward

Your prospect may try to drag out the length of the sale in order to extract more free information out of you and your competitors. Logical Customers are notorious for dragging their feet, usually to avoid the pain of change, drive a bidding war, or milk free information and concessions out of increasingly desperate salespeople.

You're not obligated to linger indefinitely.

If you've run your calls well up to this point, following the Call Flow steps, then you know how much the problem is costing your prospect, and you know the costs of delay. Bring those costs up in your conversations, for example, *"When you explained to the [Emotional Customer] that they'd have to live with an unnecessary cost of delay while you wait for the incumbent to get back to you, what was their response?"*

Here's a tip to help keep a sale moving forward when you're at the point of furnishing a proposal: Be prepared to put a tight expiration date on it. This will expedite a timely decision. Your prospect isn't entitled to the proposal's insights or offers indefinitely. On your written proposal, offer, or Statement of Work, you can simply write, "Proposal expires on" or "Valid through" with your chosen expiration date. (Ask your legal department, if you have one, for guidance.) If a Logical Customer tries to grind their internal decision-making processes to a halt for six months, they run the risk of picking up discussions again at even higher prices. There are no free moves!

Confirm No Unpaid Consulting

You're not here to provide free consulting. If the rules of the game favor your competitor (e.g., the incumbent), then you're here only to provide free insights and price pressure. You won't win.

To avoid Unpaid Consulting, you must ensure that in the presentation lineup, you're the last to present because in our experience, all else being equal, the salesperson who presents *last* will win the sale over 90% of the time.

This is why we have No-Fail Selling Rule #9: When you're not last to present, you lose.

NO-FAIL SELLING RULE #9
When you're not last to present, you lose.

This doesn't mean that if you present last, you'll win no matter what. (In addition, you can't "wimp out" at Stage 1 and then hope to win the sale by magically landing the last presentation time slot.) Rather, if you take any other time slot but last, you'll likely lose, even if you've conducted your sale skillfully up to this point.

When Terry was selling complex systems in enterprise technology, it was a condition of employment that he would be the last to present in every deal he was selling.

His sales management set that requirement because according to their stats, the last presenter won 94% of the time. Their mantra was, "If you're not last, you lose."

No matter how well you've been selling up to this point, your sale will probably get derailed if you end up presenting in any other slot but last because you're accepting a mere 6% or so chance of success.

Again, this rule doesn't guarantee a win, but it does significantly decrease the chances of losing if you're on track so far. By the time your prospect gets to the last presentation, they've seen a variety of solutions, and their questions tend to be better informed. They have a clearer idea of what's available, what they want, and what they don't want. It is not in your interest for a competitor to handle those questions.

To secure that last presentation slot, you can simply ask your prospect, *"Would there be any reason we couldn't be the last to present?"*

Tip: It's usually more effective to ask, "Would there be any reason not to?" rather than, "Could we be last to present?" It's a slightly less abrasive approach and tends to prompt more permissive answers.

Their response may illuminate something that they already know is a dealbreaker — like a heavily-favored incumbent — that's been kept under wraps until now. Funnel them down to clarity and remember that you can disrupt their process if you're willing to walk. It might sound like this:

> "That's not how we do it."
> *"That's my fault; I'm not sure I understand."*
>
> "The incumbent goes last."
> *"Maybe I'm here too early. May I tell you why I'm asking to go last, and you can tell me how we remedy that?"*

Your prospect may tell you in all honesty, "I'm afraid the other two salespeople have both tried to secure last position, and I've already let one of them have it, and I can't give it up now." In that case, the next best thing is to secure the first presentation spot — where you ensure your DV is the high bar all your other competitors have to meet — and then also secure a "final look" before they make their decision:

> *"We've found that executives like you tend to develop rich questions around this solution as they take in the options presented by the marketplace. We'll be happy to present early, but would there be any reason we couldn't touch base after the last one you see to ensure we address any new questions that have been raised in the meantime?"*

Presenting Your Solution

When you finally present your solution to your prospect, your presentation will be carefully crafted and finely tuned. To use a common sales idiom, if you simply "show up and throw up" with a one-size-fits-all pitch here, you're wimping out. Talking about your stuff is still less important than talking about your prospect's pains, so present your solution accordingly.

Subject

When you are presenting, link components of your solution directly to the things the Emotional Customer said they were seeking throughout the stages of Engage and Commit. Don't just present your solution generically — keep connecting your DV to the pains they revealed and prioritized (along with the cost of those pains) in Steps 2, 3, and 4 of your Call Flow process.

No Surprises

You must NEVER surprise the prospect at presentation time. Do not drop some "hot new technology" on them that you haven't discussed yet. You will always get a Think It Over while they shop you!

Length

Terry learned at IBM to always plan for the presentation to be done in just 50% of the allotted time. This keeps your stress levels low and provides plenty of time for input and questions from your Emotional Customers (the most important parties in the room!).

What to Cut

Trim your presentation by cutting out all the stuff about you. Your prospect's time is valuable. They do not care about your company's team culture or founding story. They do not care about you.

They do, however, care about how you can fix their pain. Talk about that.

If your company's unique team culture is what drives your DV, great — go ahead and talk about the pains it will fix; but keep the focus on the prospect, their pains, and when those pains can be fixed by your DV.

Structure

When you were uncovering your prospect's pains and motives to change through the Engage stage, you also established their priorities with regard to implementing a solution.

Your presentation will be sequenced to align with the priorities of your highest-ranking Emotional Customers. At presentation time, you will verify the prioritization given to you earlier and that there has not been a change. It sounds like this:

> *"When we spoke earlier about [Pain 1], [Pain 2], and [Pain 3], it sounded like [Pain 3] was the most critical concern to address first, with [Pain 2] close behind, and [Pain 1] a distant third. Did I hear correctly?"*

Snipers

You may find some unexpected guests in your presentation. Do not assume they are innocent bystanders; they may be supporters of a competitor who show up, collect details of your offer, and then stay silent until the Meeting After the Meeting, in which they can attack your deal more effectively.

Don't let the newcomers slip in without engaging them. Before you begin your presentation, run what we call the 2-Minute Drill with each of them. It can be done in the back of the room at the coffee station or while you're up front:

> *"I haven't had the pleasure of meeting all of you yet, but I want to make sure your agenda is included here. If we only had two minutes to address what's most important to you, what would we cover?"*

They may answer with something random intended to derail your presentation: "I just need to know you can do [and then they insert their favorite useless-but-cool-sounding thing the incumbent does]."

Stay calm, turn to the highest-ranking Emotional Customer in the room, and ask: *"That's an intriguing question, and it would take some time to address adequately here. Do you want us to pause so we can address it now, or should we wait on that and keep going with the agenda?"*

The goal is to pull the Meeting After the Meeting *into* your presentation so you do not get taken out by snipers. This is why we recommend being done with your presentation in just half of the time allotted; the rest of the time is to handle questions and snipers.

Halftime

About midway through the presentation, verify with the highest-ranking Emotional Customer in the room that you are on track. It will sound something like this:

> *"Based on what I have covered and all of our previous work, am I on track or not?"* or *"Is this addressing your needs satisfactorily?"*

If you receive anything other than a yes, funnel the answer down to clarity to determine what's missing; it may be an indicator that you slipped away from your intended agenda of covering what's most important to them and into less-relevant information about you. Shift back to being completely focused on them and their problems.

If the highest-ranking Emotional Customer indicates that they're satisfied, a sniper may still interject with something negative in an attempt to pull you down a rabbit hole where they'll test your technical competence: "Well, I'm not convinced you can do [whatever the incumbent can do]." Simply turn to your Emotional Customer and ask: *"Should we park it here, or keep going?"* Let them be the one to decide whether or not to take the sniper seriously.

They'll usually want to keep going, but in the event they give the sniper room to take shots at you, simply bring everything back to the priorities on the table and the cost of delay:

> *"It sounds like priorities have changed, and that's my fault. It'll take some time to explore this, so please help me understand what the new date is for when you need to see revenue coming in from this upgrade."*

When You're Done Presenting

When you finish presenting an offer to do business, ask your prospect for the decision they committed to make.

> *"I'd like to make sure that I understand where we are and that we've addressed your questions. So let's imagine a scale from zero to ten, with zero being 'there's no way this thing will ever see the light of day again' and ten being you've decided this is the solution you want. What would be an accurate number based on what you've seen so far?"*

Note the nuance here: your scale is *zero* to ten, not *one* to ten. This is so important in respecting your prospect's autonomy! A ONE-to-ten scale doesn't give them the option to kill this deal. Don't take that option away from them. They have the right to kill this deal, so make sure your scale is *zero* to ten, or you'll inadvertently irritate them with the trap close.

If it's under seven, take the loss gracefully. *"Sounds like we're done."*

If it's seven to nine, you can ask: *"Sounds like we may have missed a few gaps. What would you need to see or hear from us to get above that number?"*

If it's a ten, you have a clear indication from your prospect that they will recommend you in the Meeting After the Meeting. In that case, you can expect a phone call shortly confirming that you've won the business.

Securing Your Win

You won! Congratulations ... but you're not out of the woods yet. This is the place where many salespeople get blindsided by sudden unexpected changes in heart and mind. You must prepare for inevitable competitive reactions, both internal and external, to avoid any nasty surprises here.

Every sale is competitive — that is, there are always competitors in the race with you, ready to take the business away from you. Even if your only competitor is the status quo favored by the Logical Customer, it's still a competitor. Your questions throughout your selling conversations — especially around their process to evaluate and decide on a solution — helped you get a strategic view of the competitive landscape, and you probably have a pretty good idea of who your primary competitor is in this sale.

When you are advised you have won, you must reconfirm it. Don't throw your victory party yet. The winner always gets notified first; it's the more pleasant phone call, and human nature tends to prioritize the pleasant. The losers will be notified next — and you need to count on a loser appealing for another look. They may announce some hot new technology or a last-minute break-through that will allow them to reprice their original offer.

To strengthen your win with some victory insurance, address the possibility of competitive reactions with your prospect. Do this when they're notifying you that you won the business:

- Anticipate how your prospect will react to a last-minute pitch from your competition.
- Discuss with your prospect how they will handle that pitch; you can even practice what the conversation will sound like together.
- Reestablish their commitment to you.

Here's what it might sound like:

> *"What do you think Brand X will do when they find out you've decided to make a change?"*
> *"How do you plan to react or deal with that?"*
> *"What is your view of the final outcome of those discussions?"*

The competitive reactions could come from outsiders who were also competing for the business or from within the prospect organization (for example, the Logical Customer who's disgruntled because they've been overridden, or the guy on the Board who'd promised his buddy the business but got outvoted).

Either way, if you anticipate and prepare for the backlash with these simple questions, you're more likely to thwart their efforts and keep your win secure.

We once helped a client — let's call them UpStart, Inc. — win a piece of business with a large prospect for the first time. UpStart, Inc. was relatively small, and they had been competing against a large, established enterprise for the business. It was a difficult and competitive sale. UpStart, Inc. moved with agility and leveraged their DV throughout the sale very effectively, especially in the last few days of the prospect's decision-making process.

Unbeknownst to us, their competitor was so convinced this deal was secure that they had already booked a private room at a local restaurant to celebrate their win. (They hadn't learned about fiction-free forecasting yet!) When the phone call announcing their loss to UpStart, Inc. came in, the celebration had already started, and the drinks were freely flowing. The party quickly turned into a wake.

Don't underestimate the speed, agility, or skills of your competitors; make sure you're leveraging your DV all the way through the close of the sale, and work with your prospect to secure your win even once they've made their decision in your favor.

Launch onboarding transition

The cast of characters you engaged throughout your complex sale was likely an ad hoc group within the prospect organization; this group will disintegrate after the decision is made, and everyone will go back to their normal work.

Now, that decision to do business with you will ripple down to the employees charged with making the project successful. This means the work of implementing your solution will probably be handed off to … the Logical Customer.

This is the Logical Customer who gets an email one Friday afternoon from their executive telling them effectively, "Hey, on

Monday you'll meet a team who will help you do a much better job."

Do not underestimate the hostility you (or your account managers) will encounter in this phase. This Logical Customer does not become your friend just because they're assigned to help you implement your solution. They will give the illusion of cooperation but may quietly drag their feet in hopes that the project will crash. If that happens, expect passive-aggressive behavior here. They think they already have good methodology for the implementation and don't want to make any changes. And they're probably feeling especially Not OK because the Emotional Customer exerted their authority and economic power.

To prepare for this possibility, look back at your cast of characters and ask yourself, who was cool and noncommittal during your sale? That's probably a passive-aggressive Logical Customer who didn't get what they want, and they may drag their feet during implementation. We have clients who serve large capital projects, and they regularly encounter project managers who intentionally delay each project's improvement, deferring progress by being nonresponsive or muddying the waters with lies that take considerable time to sort out.

Therefore, even after you've landed your account, be prepared to engage the Logical Customers carefully and gracefully during implementation, in all the ways we've been advising you to engage them throughout your sale. Stay Not OK. Ask questions that pull in the Emotional Customer's agenda into the conversation. Ensure the cost of delay is on the table at all times. Plan to handle their stalls and pushbacks, just like you did in Chapter 7, with humility and efficiency.

On your side, work with your team to ensure that all parties involved in onboarding this new customer understand the importance of staying Not OK in all conversations. This is usually the time when brilliant subject-matter experts get involved in the implementation process, and they may inadvertently call your client incompetent or alienate reluctant Logical Customers, blowing up fragile rapport during implementation.

Make sure everyone involved — subject-matter experts, operations, IT, client success, and account managers — is equipped with the conversational skills necessary to keep the implementation moving forward with your new client's goodwill.

Secure for the long term

You probably engaged an Emotional Customer at or near the executive level over the course of your sale. You determined the pains and consequences that this Executive wanted fixed, in a particular order of importance.

Once the sale is complete and your solution is chosen, the Executive moves on to other pressing problems. They hand their decision off for implementation, and another department becomes responsible for putting your solution into play.

During that time, though, your Emotional Customer is being called on by other sellers. They are being listed on someone else's forecast. To secure your deal so that it survives competitive assaults for a long time, do one small thing: As soon as your implementation team declares that the goals most important to the Executive have been achieved, contact that Executive and run a conversation like this:

> *"When you made the decision to work with us, your top three priorities were [1 ... 2 ... 3]. My people believe implementation has addressed them; we've checked with your people, and they agree. But none of that matters if you don't agree, so what's your opinion?"*

The Executive will remember this; hardly anyone ever comes back full circle to make sure their goals were fully satisfied after implementation. They often bring you the next big problem they have that needs solving. In addition, they may also tell their friends in peer groups (serving on boards together, volunteering together, hanging out in golf and yacht clubs) about you, and you will gain valuable referrals from your work together.

CHAPTER TEN

Ongoing Selling and Forecasting

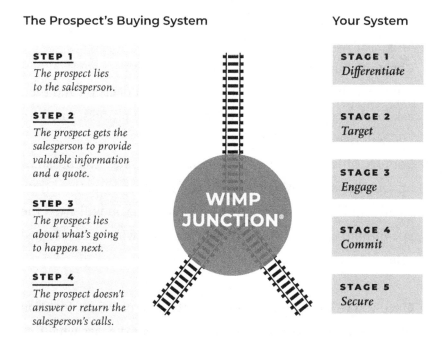

The Prospect's Buying System

STEP 1
The prospect lies to the salesperson.

STEP 2
The prospect gets the salesperson to provide valuable information and a quote.

STEP 3
The prospect lies about what's going to happen next.

STEP 4
The prospect doesn't answer or return the salesperson's calls.

WIMP JUNCTION®

Your System

STAGE 1
Differentiate

STAGE 2
Target

STAGE 3
Engage

STAGE 4
Commit

STAGE 5
Secure

Congratulations! You've successfully navigated your complex sale through the five stages that help you avoid Wimp Junction. In quick summary, these five stages are:

1. **Differentiate:** This is the foundation for everything else that follows. When you differentiate yourself strategically in the marketplace, you sound different from all the other sellers who are calling on your prospects, and you protect yourself from commoditization.

2. **Target:** This allows you to reach the right players in the cast of characters. When you leverage your DV to reach the Emotional Customers, you will land more conversations with the people who can help your opportunity move forward.

3. **Engage:** This is where you carry your DV the Last Mile in conversations to overcome isolation at your prospect organization. When you keep the cost of delay front and center, your opportunities will accelerate.

4. **Commit:** This is the hardest stage for most salespeople. When you clarify how your prospect will make their decision and then ask for their commitment to follow their own process, your win rate will rise significantly.

5. **Secure:** This is so much more than the old sales idiom, "show up and throw up." When you approach your presentation strategically, and you know what will happen next, you will avoid the last-minute risks that can sabotage an otherwise well-executed sale.

Once you've closed an opportunity, the risk of Wimp Junction is still very high! It never really goes away. Let's discuss what that risk looks like during and after implementation as well as strategies to avoid Wimp Junction once you're in an account.

STAY OUT OF WIMP JUNCTION: *Account Management*

The easiest sale in the world is the one you've already won — but that doesn't mean there won't be new threats.

Congratulations on making it all the way through a complex sale without wimping out! You followed the tracks all the way down to securing your sale. Let's talk about what happens now.

After a complex sale is won, the role of Client Success Manager (or Account Manager) becomes critically important. The Client Success Manager is charged with protecting this valuable, hard-earned new revenue stream. They must master the skills and mindset required in this selling system because they will continue selling to the client long after the deal has been closed.

We cannot overestimate the importance of skilled account management. This Client Success Manager may be the same hunter who closed the deal, or it may be a farmer to whom the account has been transferred. Either way, they must continue selling even after the deal is won — because competitors (internal and external) are always circling, ready to convince your client to move away.

Always remember one critical truth: Your best customer is listed right now on someone else's forecast. The lifetime value of a customer, and the cost of acquiring a new customer, are both high enough to justify attentive and continued selling to protect the existing revenue stream.

Over the life of this account, your client's company will change. Owners will retire. Consultants will be hired. New leaders will replace departing leaders. New systems will render old processes obsolete. Strategies will shift. There will be key internal changes to their decision-making structure.

Wimp Junction is still a risk, even now — and it is the difference between reactive and proactive account management.

Reactive account management

After a sale has concluded in a win, it's easy to get comfortable for a while. All parties are satisfied. Your solution is working. Some people change roles, new players come in, but everything keeps humming along. You reasonably anticipate that when your contract is up for renewal, your customer will renew the business.

REACTIVE ACCOUNT MANAGEMENT

But suddenly, when your contract is up for renewal, you find yourself receiving an RFP from your customer. They've opened up your business to competitors! You go into "React Mode" as you attempt to sell your value and escape the bidding war.

But by that point, the selling window — your opportunity to sell your value in this client relationship — has closed. The selling window closes when the RFP is issued (or when an outside consultant takes control of the purchase process). The decision will be deliberated in a black hole of silence until the contract is issued to the lowest bidder.

NO-FAIL RULE #10
If you didn't create the specifications for the RFP,
you are column fodder.

No matter how smoothly your relationship has been humming along until now, you will be commoditized if you end up responding to an RFP or RFQ that you didn't help create.

Sometimes you can't avoid a client issuing RFPs, such as when it's required by law. But you can have a say in what the RFP requires — and you need to make sure that it recognizes and values your points of Differentiating Value (DV).

You must understand your customer's decision-making process (which might have changed since you won the business) and the stakeholders involved (who also might have changed), and sell your DV so it remains valued more highly than a competitor's lower price or other features.

The only time to accomplish that is when the selling window is open — long before an RFP is issued or outside consultants take control — with proactive account management.

Proactive account management

Proactive account management is simply selling into your client relationship while the selling window is open so that your points of Differentiating Value are recognized and valued in your client's next decision-making process. It looks like this:

PROACTIVE ACCOUNT MANAGEMENT

Essentially, the Client Success Manager or Account Manager must start selling into the relationship right away — that is, checking in and having conversations with Emotional Customers to ensure your DV remains valued more highly than someone else's lower price or other features. This isn't the same as upselling, where we sell more to the same client (although that's a good goal too) — this is simply defensive work to maintain ground we've already won.

Approach this selling window like a salesperson pursuing a complex sale, using the techniques you've learned in this selling system.

Here is an illustration of the information you must gather while this selling window is open; you'll recognize much from the steps of our selling system. In this case, you're simply applying it to managing an existing account rather than winning a new deal:

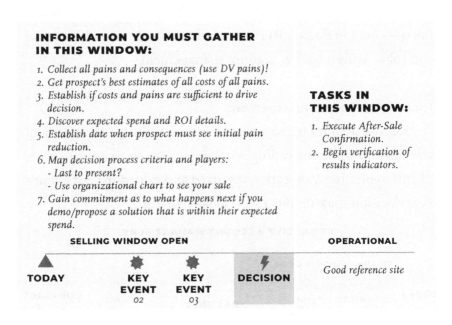

INFORMATION YOU MUST GATHER IN THIS WINDOW:

1. *Collect all pains and consequences (use DV pains)!*
2. *Get prospect's best estimates of all costs of all pains.*
3. *Establish if costs and pains are sufficient to drive decision.*
4. *Discover expected spend and ROI details.*
5. *Establish date when prospect must see initial pain reduction.*
6. *Map decision process criteria and players:*
   - *Last to present?*
   - *Use organizational chart to see your sale*
7. *Gain commitment as to what happens next if you demo/propose a solution that is within their expected spend.*

TASKS IN THIS WINDOW:

1. *Execute After-Sale Confirmation.*
2. *Begin verification of results indicators.*

SELLING WINDOW OPEN — OPERATIONAL

TODAY — KEY EVENT 02 — KEY EVENT 03 — DECISION — *Good reference site*

Don't wimp out by settling in with their implementation team. Keep your routes to the Emotional Customer open; stay on top of the org chart changes. Learn what's important to whom. Keep selling your value using the techniques you've learned in this selling system.

"Nerdley"

The following chart shows the relationship between the elevation of your contacts at your client enterprise and your margins.

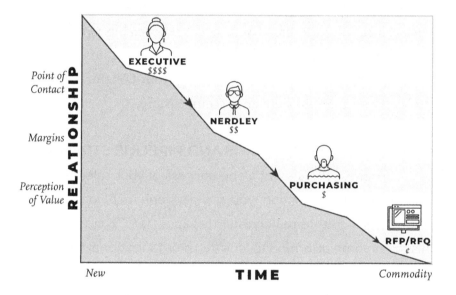

At the beginning of your client relationship, your primary contact is probably your high-ranking Emotional Customer who values your DV, and your margins are high.

But you'll get handed off to "Nerdley" (our affectionate name for the Logical Customer who's usually a subject-matter expert) for implementation, and Nerdley will become your primary contact. This is the beginning of a dangerous downward slide toward commodity status, and the gravitational pull is strong.

Nerdley's job is to conflate price and cost. At some point over the course of your business relationship, Nerdley will probably declare that what you're selling is a total commodity and that your "great service," "wonderful people," "responsiveness," and "great technology" are simply table stakes to be on the RFP list.

In time, as Nerdley leaves the company to go work on their PhD, you may find yourself sliding even further down to Purchasing, Procurement, or Supply Chain Management, and responding to RFPs online. At that point, your margins (and job security) are gone.

It's critical over the life of your client relationship to maintain communication with your Emotional Customers and to continually leverage the consequences of not having your DV; this will help you keep your margins high and account secure.

KEEP LONG-TERM MARGINS AND PIPELINE STRENGTH

As you improve the cadence and success of your sales by staying out of Wimp Junction, you can also enhance your organization's sales culture to consistently expect a 90% closing rate. This takes some attention to long-term organizational habits:

1. Refreshing your Differentiating Value (DV) regularly
2. Fiction-free forecasting
3. Differentiating strategically in unique competitive situations

Refreshing Your DV

Today's competitive advantage is tomorrow's table stakes. After all the work you've done in previous chapters to determine and articulate your Differentiating Value (DV), you may be tempted to enshrine the results for posterity and consider the task done forever.

Unfortunately, DV is dynamic and ever-changing, and you must plan to refresh your DV often — at least every year, and probably a few times a year if you're in a fast-changing industry. Your competitors are always close behind you, trying to close the gap. The marketplace is always changing, and your prospects are evolving.

Stay agile by refreshing your DV strategically at least once a year. Dig in to determine what sets you apart from your competitors in the marketplace in each new season. What sets you apart? Is your DV the first or second flavor? What's changed? Run the DV exercise strategically with fresh eyes at least once a year, and maybe even semi-annually or quarterly to stay agile.

Additionally, make sure your salespeople (especially new hires) run the DV exercise themselves before hitting the street. The thought required to articulate DV helps accomplish the necessary tectonic shift in salespeople's thinking, from talking to prospects about us to talking to prospects about them instead. We start all our work with salespeople by running them through the DV exercise tactically (which we shared with you in Chapter 4).

Having your salespeople run the DV exercise themselves also helps them unearth DV language unique to them. The DV exercise produces "gold nuggets" of language that become the substance of conversations with prospects, and it's critical that salespeople internalize this language and are comfortable using it. For this reason, we strongly suggest having all salespeople run the DV exercise tactically so they produce language that they can personally leverage in their own conversations with prospects.

FORECASTING AND PIPELINE REVIEWS

Sales forecasting is a thorn in the side of many CFOs, revenue officers, and sales managers. Too many forecasts are built on hope without solid metrics to determine the true likelihood of success. But your sales forecasts can be accurate if you know which metrics to measure.

A milestone-centric sales process (like collecting the nine Attributes of a Qualified Selling Opportunity) feeds an accurate forecast. Here are the ways we help our clients achieve fiction-free forecasts.

Target titles

We always begin by clarifying the difference between leads, suspects, and prospects because you must distinguish them in order to build an accurate forecast.

- **Leads** are just the names of your targets. You're planning to get their contact info and to contact them.
- **Suspects** are your leads for whom you have acquired reliable contact information. Perhaps you've even started talking to them. But they're still just suspects, not prospects, because they haven't yet indicated any motives to change.
- **Prospects** are your suspects who have admitted to having clear motives to change.

Until *you've heard* a target admit that they have motives to change, you do not have a prospect. You cannot call a suspect a prospect just because, according to you, they have reasons to change. Those reasons don't count until you've heard them come out of your suspect's mouth — not yours.

Keep this critical distinction in mind when planning your forecast. Knowing they have reasons to change isn't enough to call a target a prospect; you must hear *them* express their motive to change in order to count them as a prospect on your forecast here.

Real motivation to change is the price of admission onto your forecast. All your other new targets are either leads or suspects.

A prospect will remain a prospect on the forecast until the deal is closed; at that point they become a *customer.* Customers are listed on your sales forecast when they offer a new business opportunity.

These four definitions here are tighter than they typically are in conversation. When we talk casually about opportunities in general, we may call all of our targets "prospects." But when it comes to accurate forecasting, we strongly recommend tightening up the language to distinguish between leads, suspects, prospects, and customers. This will help you keep fiction out of your pipeline meetings, as the tight definitions tend to bring more clarity about where an opportunity really is in discussion.

The five stages to track opportunities

To help you avoid hitting Wimp Junction in your sale, we offer five stages to follow on the right side of the train tracks. Here's what the complete flow looks like with the steps to take in each stage:

- **Differentiate** yourself in this opportunity
  - DV Exercise done
- **Target** the right prospects using your DV
  - ECs identified proactively
  - 30-Second Infomercial crafted for initial conversations
  - Voicemail-Email Pairing System crafted for outreach
  - Further outreach planned (with collateral lined up)
- **Engage** the right prospects and leverage your DV: (Call Flow 1–6)

1. Gain agreement to the sales process.
2. Collect multiple pains from the prospect.
3. Confirm the order of importance of prospect's pains.
4. Drill down to extract all costs of pains and problems.
5. Confirm that adequate resources are available.
6. Draw out the exact date to begin harvesting the benefits of a solution.

- **Commit** to next steps with your prospect: (Call Flow 7–9)

7. Confirm that their evaluation and decision-making processes are understood.
8. Agree on clear outcomes with prospect.
9. Attain mutual agreement to move forward.

- **Secure** the sale:
  - Once all nine Attributes have been collected, we present an offer to do business and secure the sale.

We strongly recommend using these five stages to track each opportunity in progress. They can be easily built into your CRM and can feed your forecast.

The first two stages (Differentiate and Target) may seem like big-picture strategic planning to be done once and checked off for a while. However, they should be evaluated for every opportunity you pursue. The DV you leverage will be unique to each opportunity, and you want to make sure you're strategically targeting the right people in the cast of characters with the right language. Do your homework and complete these planning stages for each opportunity you pursue. If they're skipped, you risk being commoditized by the wrong targets and landing at Wimp Junction in the later stages of your sale.

The final three stages (Engage, Commit, and Secure) are where the tactical execution of the sales process happens. This is where we collect the nine Attributes of a Qualified Selling Opportunity in the nine steps of our Call Flow process to determine if this is an opportunity we can win at an acceptable investment of our time and resources. Then, we secure the sale.

Translating Attributes to forecast

The Attributes of a Qualified Selling Opportunity (QSO) will drive your fiction-free sales forecast. The probability that your deal will be won increases as you move through your Call Flow and the Attributes are satisfied one by one.

Remember, the Call Flow steps make both a micro process (the flow of a single conversation) and a macro process (the flow of your sale as you collect Attributes from multiple conversations with multiple parties).

Naturally, there's room to make the adjustments necessary to your business. We have clients in high-tech enterprise sales who further qualify their opportunities with technical requirements at their prospect organizations, so they add more Attributes to their checklist. We have other clients who simplify our nine Attributes to a simple list of a half-dozen boxes that are checked off in a couple of conversations with laser focus at the right altitude.

As you make any necessary adjustments, however, please keep in mind that the order of the steps is intentional and strategic. We strongly recommend following the order we've laid out here because jumping around will cost you additional time and effort. For example, jumping to Step 5 (Confirm Adequate Resources) before you've extracted all the costs of the problem in Step 4 (Drill

Down) will stall your opportunity as the conversation jumps ahead to price, and you'll hit Wimp Junction.

As you track the collection of the Attributes of a Qualified Selling Opportunity, you'll have increased situational awareness: You will know exactly where in your sales process each opportunity is in its progression toward closure. You will also know its likelihood of closure based on the Attributes collected so far.

How we translate Attributes into a simple and clear forecast

For the sake of visual simplicity when forecasting, we combine some steps into a single factor on the forecast. For example, the first four Call Flow steps all relate to collecting actionable enterprise pain and drilling down to full clarity on the costs and consequences of not having our DV, so they're combined into one factor: actionable pain.

Some factors contribute more to the likelihood of closure than others. For this reason, we recommend weighting them as follows once they are in your pipeline:

Your opportunity in the **Engage** stage:

- **Actionable pains identified:** 30% likelihood of closure when this is complete
  - Multiple enterprise pains have been collected and drilled down to full clarity around what the enterprise is spending each day they don't have our DV. (We recommend 10% for each pain collected, up to three pains.)
  - This forecast factor maps to these Call Flow Steps:
    - » *Call Flow 1: Gain agreement to the sales process.*
    - » *Call Flow 2: Collect multiple pains from the prospect.*

> » *Call Flow 3: Confirm the order of importance of prospect's pains.*
> » *Call Flow 4: Drill down to extract all costs of pains and problems.*

- **Expected spend uncovered and funded:** 10% likelihood of closure when this is complete
  - Prospect has discussed the expected spend to fix the problem, and we know that funding is available. (We recommend awarding 5% for uncovering the prospect's expected spend to fix the problem and 5% for verifying that funding is available.)
  - This forecast factor maps to *Call Flow 5: Confirm Adequate Resources.*
- **Date identified to harvest benefits:** 5% likelihood of closure when this is complete
  - Prospect has identified the date they want to begin harvesting the benefits of a solution to their problem. (While this could be combined into the "actionable pain" factor, we recommend leaving it separate because it is so critical to closure.)
  - This forecast factor maps to *Call Flow 6: Draw out the exact date to begin harvesting the benefits of a solution.*

Your opportunity in the **Commit** stage:
- **Evaluation and decision-making processes are understood:** 35% likelihood of closure when this is complete
  - We have uncovered the processes they use to evaluate and decide on a solution like this, and we know where we'll get points for our DV. (We recommend requiring at least three Emotional Customers in the cast of characters here. Sales that rely on single-channel communication often stall unnecessarily.)

- This forecast factor maps to *Call Flow 7: Confirm that their evaluation and decision-making processes are understood.*

♦ **Gain commitment to move forward:** 10% likelihood of closure when this is complete
  - We know exactly what will happen next if and when we put an offer on the table.
  - This forecast factor maps to these Call Flow Steps:
    » *Call Flow 8: Agree on clear outcomes with prospect.*
    » *Call Flow 9: Attain mutual agreement to move forward.*

Your opportunity in the **Secure** stage:

♦ **Present and secure:** 10% likelihood of closure when this is complete
  - We present our solution and an offer to do business, and we secure the sale. We recommend awarding 5% for presenting the solution and offer to do business, and awarding another 5% for securing the sale against competitive assaults.

Please note that the first factor that puts an opportunity onto the forecast is actionable pain; it is effectively the price of admission to get onto your forecast.

In summary, here are the six forecast factors we recommend and their weights based on the Call Flow steps to collect the Attributes of a Qualified Selling Opportunity:

♦ Actionable pain identified: 30%
♦ Expected spend uncovered and funded: 10%
♦ Date identified to harvest benefits: 5%

◆ Evaluation and decision-making processes are understood: 35%

◆ Commitment gained to move forward: 10%

◆ Presented and secured: 10%

This weighted approach accounts for the Attributes of a QSO when evaluating the probability of success, increasing the accuracy of the forecast. "They sound really interested" is no longer a contributing factor. Your CFO will thank you.

Pipeline reviews

Sales leaders: When you review your forecast with your team, here are a few questions we recommend asking to keep fiction from creeping into the conversation:

1. What Attributes have you collected?

2. When you say you've collected that Attribute, is it because the prospect SAID something to confirm it or because you guessed? (Guessing doesn't count — only the prospect's actual words count as truth!)

3. What Attributes do you still have to collect?

4. How will you collect them? (If the salesperson says anything like, "I'll explain ..." or "I'll tell them about our DV," that's a red light — Wimp Junction ahead!)

5. What's the next action you and the prospect agreed to? (You must have mutual agreement to move forward. "They've agreed to think it over for a while" doesn't count as action!)

Competitive Situation Analysis

One of our favorite consulting exercises with clients is Competitive Situation Analysis. This exercise gathers what you've learned with us and applies it with laser focus to a single situation against a single competitor: either one high-stakes deal, or one corner of the marketplace where you regularly encounter that competitor.

Terry first developed this process when he was a young man selling complex enterprise technology solutions. Though his solutions were technologically superior, they had a price tag 80% higher than the nearest competitors and a two-year delivery time (compared to the competitor's ninety days). Sales were difficult. Competitive analysis was key to being successful, and he won often.

This process has since been through several revisions and is now used and taught in approximately 2,000 of our client companies.

The essence of the process is the application of No-Fail Selling Rule #1: All business decisions involve tradeoffs, and tradeoffs have consequences. There are no free moves.

This simple, four-step analysis will help you identify what the prospect finds appealing in a competitor's offer, what the tradeoffs will be if the prospect does not select you, and the consequences of the tradeoffs. It sounds easy but requires some thought.

You will also be guided to the most effective positioning questions to ask to see if your prospect values the things you bring to them that are either unique to you, or if not unique, you can demonstrate that you execute better and are the better value.

In the analysis of a particular competitive sales situation, you may analyze a type of competitor at a high level across a market, or you may analyze a competitor in a contest at a specific account. This approach is extremely effective in both situations.

There are four simple steps:

1. Answer this question in as much detail as possible:

What does the prospect get or gain if they buy from the competition? List everything the *prospect* would use to justify their decision. Their perspective is what matters here, not yours.

Note: Sometimes when we are teaching this, we see salespeople and their leaders try to list the negative things the prospect will also be getting. Don't bother. We will cover those things more effectively in Step Two.

_____

_____

_____

2. Answer this question in as much detail as possible:

If the prospect picks the competitor who offers those benefits we just listed, what does the prospect give up that is either unique or demonstrably better in our offer? List everything they give up when they don't do business with you, whether or not they are aware of it or value it at this time.

_____

_____

_____

Maybe your list includes quality, service, support, and great people. That's a good start, and every competitor you have has that list. And as soon as two competing sellers are saying the same thing, the prospect quickly concludes, "It's a commodity, let's start the auction," and now your margins go virtual.

Focus on whatever is unique or demonstrably better in your offer compared to your competitor's in this situation.

If you find yourself stuck here, try asking yourself this question: What do you wish the market valued more highly (or at all) about your offer? In other words, what is something they just don't "get" or don't see as important?

What you've just identified is something that if the market valued, your sales would close more easily, and your margins would be higher. So what is it you offer that you wish the market understood and valued? Those are the "give-ups" you're listing here in Step Two.

3. So what?

If you just talk about the things you listed in Step Two, the prospect will silently be asking, "So what?" So keep going in Step Three to refine your language so the prospect doesn't have to ask, "So what?" to understand how it applies to them.

Step Two is about you. Step Three is about them. Which do you think is more interesting to them?

Take each give-up that you listed in Step Two and filter it through these questions:

- How would not having it show up in their life? (If it truly has value, then not having it truly has consequences!)
- When would it show up?

- Who would feel it when it showed up?
- Who would get the bill if there were costs associated with the give-up?

_____

_____

_____

Naturally, at this step, you've just identified the Emotional Customers (your natural allies when you want to sell on value and not price). Make sure your Emotional Customers are engaged!

4. At this point, you can position your value optimally.
You will have flexibility to adapt your message to different situations as required. Simply take the consequences of the give-up from Step Three and put them into play by inserting them into any one of the three effective opening question formats we discussed in Chapter 7.

- Format 1: Negative Opening Comment + 1-Sentence story + Open-Ended Question
- Format 2: Negative Opening Comment + Assumptive question ("When you ... ?" or "The last time ... ?")
- Format 3: Negative Opening Comment + Two-choice question

To review, Format 1 is a great all-purpose tool to introduce your value to the prospect. Format 2 is useful when you're up against an entrenched competitor who's probably vulnerable because they're underserving. And Format 3 efficiently puts two of your DV points into play at the same time.

These questions will be laser-focused on your DV for this prospect in this competitive situation and will help you leverage your unique value against this particular competitor to win the business.

Do this exercise with your sales team. Understand what is appealing in your competitor's offer — truly appealing, from the prospect's perspective. Understand what it costs your prospect to pick your competitor. Compare your answers. Practice the questions on each other. Then, you'll be ready to face the competition.

Epilogue

THE SALE, REIMAGINED

You've been pursuing this opportunity for months. You meticulously researched the enterprise and their needs. You prospected; you networked; you got past gatekeepers. You landed various meetings with different role players ...

And in each conversation, you asked strategic questions to leverage your unique Differentiating Value, qualify your opportunity, and drive your DV into their decision-making process.

You ran through the Call Flow steps in every conversation with all the players in the cast of characters. You methodically collected the Attributes of a Qualified Selling Opportunity to determine that this prospect enterprise does, in fact, have actionable pain, and that this is an opportunity you can win.

Your skillfully-asked questions in every conversation caused the other person to talk for 80% of each call, allowing you to collect valuable information about the prospect enterprise and all the ways they're paying to not do business with you right now.

Those costs and consequences became the currency of the realm to measure pain, value, and your competitors' offers.

You encountered Logical Customers along the way who told you they'd need some time to confer, compare, and learn a bit more about your solution before moving on to next steps. You effortlessly pulled the Emotional Customer's agenda into each conversation so that the cost of delay remained front and center. They suddenly didn't need another demonstration to think it over.

You learned about the process they would use to evaluate and decide on a solution provider, and you influenced it to value your unique differentiators over someone else's lower price. You saw how the decision would be ultimately resolved by the Board of Directors, so you learned what was most important to them and equipped your Emotional Customer to make the case in favor of your solution. You leveraged the cost of delay at every turn.

When it came time to present your solution and your offer to do business, you wisely concluded that each unexpected meeting attendee wasn't just there to get out of the rain and that they probably had an agenda that might be hostile. You ran the 2-Minute Drill to smoke out what was most important to each person. Sure enough, there was a sniper: a disgruntled Logical Customer whose buddy at the incumbent provider hadn't yet been able to solve this problem. Their hyper-technical question challenged your solution's capabilities and almost pulled the entire meeting down a rabbit hole. Luckily, you deferred to the Emotional Customer, who decided that question could be shelved for now, and your presentation proceeded without interference.

Before leaving the meeting, you asked your prospect for the decision they'd committed to make; thus, you knew before returning to your office exactly what their recommendation to the Board would be and what next steps would look like. You strategized with your Emotional Customer to handle the most likely competitive reactions (especially from that disgruntled sniper), and they valued your consultative insights.

When you learned that you won the business, you took great satisfaction in moving the opportunity forward in your CRM.

But really, it wasn't a surprise to anyone.

WIMP JUNCTION: THE PLACE A SALE IS LOST

The moment you begin pursuing an opportunity, your sale is in motion. Your sale has left its station and is moving along its tracks.

Throughout your sale, you will find yourself facing Wimp Junction many times. There, you will choose to either follow the prospect's buying system — where everything is commoditized and margins go up in smoke — or follow your selling system, where you can consistently sell at high value in less time.

The five stages we've shared with you here will help you stay on the right side of the tracks and avoid being pulled down to the prospect's side of the tracks.

The Differentiate stage comes first; if you can get full clarity around your Differentiating Value (DV) for this prospect in this opportunity, then your sale is solidly positioned on your side of the tracks. But if you skip this stage, it's a one-way ticket to Wimp Junction.

When you use your DV to Target the right prospects in Stage 2, you'll stay on your tracks and will put some distance between your sale and the Logical Customers who seek to commoditize you at Wimp Junction.

In Stage 3, Engage, you'll engage the right prospects using the Communication Keys we've provided to collect the Attributes of a Qualified Selling Opportunity (QSO); this will keep you from providing Unpaid Consulting at Wimp Junction.

Stage 4, Commit, is the stage at which Wimp Junction is perhaps most difficult to avoid, but getting clarity around your prospect's processes to evaluate and decide on your solution, and getting commitment to mutually-agreed-upon next steps, will keep you on track.

In Stage 5, Secure, you'll stay on your side of the tracks with ruthless honesty around which Attributes of a QSO you've collected so far and with vigilance around competitive threats when it's time to present your offer to do business.

In essence, these tracks tell you where you are in your process and what to do next. These tracks provide enhanced situational awareness and clarity to move forward and win the opportunity at high value.

Ever since our founding nearly forty years ago, our goal at Slattery has been to empower our clients to win more sales — faster, and at higher margins. We want to equip them to engage the marketplace with humility and integrity. And we want to see them earn more for their enterprises, their families, and the causes that need their support.

In our experience, sales tends to be one corner of the marketplace where there are mercifully few barriers to entry — you don't need a wealthy background, connected family, or advanced degrees to get started in sales. And the sky's the limit for success and financial growth.

Not many people are willing to do the beautiful, important, and often difficult work of persuading other humans to change what they're doing, with both their cooperation and consent. But those who do can find great personal success, and make the world a better place at the same time.

It's a privilege to help equip you for that work and for further success. The concept of Wimp Junction has helped thousands of salespeople and leaders get stuck deals moving again toward closure at high value, and ultimately lifted their sales career entirely. We hope we've done the same for you.

Thank you.

Glossary

1-Sentence Story *An effective tool to weave the power of storytelling into your conversations with prospects, the 1-Sentence Story affirms that your prospect is not alone in their struggles and builds your credibility by highlighting your experience in the marketplace. (Anything longer than one sentence is probably too long!)*

2-Minute Drill *A brief interaction with unexpected attendees at your presentation who often arrive at the scheduled time and leave before you're done, the 2-Minute Drill helps clarify their priorities and gives you a chance to handle any objections they may raise now.*

30-Second Infomercial *A planned statement or message entirely focused on your ideal target — the Emotional Customer — that translates your DV to their world in thirty seconds or less.*

80/20 Rule *The rule that a seller should be listening for 80% of the time and talking for 20% of the time during sales calls. (The talking 20%*

should be spent asking strategic questions to prompt answers, remaining consultative, and collecting information.)

Actionable pain *Pain that hurts badly enough to outweigh the pain of change and overcome our natural resistance to it. Actionable pain is not mere interest — it is powerful motivation to change.*

Attributes *The Attributes of a Qualified Selling Opportunity are the nine pieces of data you need to uncover about an opportunity to maintain a 90% closing rate.*

B2B *Business-to-business sales; that is, one enterprise selling to another enterprise.*

Buying System *The prospect's process and methods to evaluate and decide on new vendors and solutions. Many enterprise buyers are trained to view vendors as commodities and to extract discounts and concessions through their buying system.*

Call Flow *The orderly progression through the steps of your sales calls to collect the Attributes of a Qualified Selling Opportunity (QSO) one by one.*

Cast of Characters *The various stakeholders within your prospect organization who are involved in your sale, including all the people who have input during the evaluation and decision-making processes, and may also include others who don't vote but can either help support or sabotage your sale along the way.*

Cinnamon Question *What's happening to whom at your prospect organization because they are not your customer?*

Client Success Manager or Account Manager *The person tasked with managing the relationship with the prospect after the sale has successfully closed and the prospect has become a client. This person might be the same seller who closed the deal, or it might be a different person. They must continue selling to avoid Wimp Junction in the future.*

Closed-Ended Question *A question that prompts a yes-or-no answer. Any question beginning with words like could, would, are, or did is a closed-ended question.*

Cognitive dissonance *Inconsistency between one's thoughts or attitudes and their behavior; in other words, believing or saying one thing while doing another. Often shows up in Logical Customers who have been masquerading as Emotional Customers when you ask them to agree to next steps.*

Commoditization *The process of being commoditized — i.e., being treated as a commodity, as if what you offer is totally interchangeable with your competitors' offerings. In commodity sales, there is high pressure for discounts and concessions. When all else is equal, lowest price will win.*

Competitive Situation Analysis *An exercise we run with clients to gather your DV work and apply it with laser focus to a single situation against a single competitor: either one high-stakes deal or one corner of the marketplace where you regularly encounter that competitor.*

Complex sale *A sale that involves multiple buying parties and multiple discussions. This is different from a simple sale that can be completed in a single transaction.*

Congruent *A person who is congruent believes what they're saying. If they're not congruent, then the other person's nervous system will pick up on tiny triggers alerting them to the incongruence, and trust will be lost. A seller must always be congruent.*

Cost of delay *The cost experienced by your prospect enterprise for every month, week, or even day they delay adopting your solution and taking advantage of all that your DV could be doing for them.*

Differentiating Value (DV) *Your unique edge that differentiates you from your competition and is valued by your prospects so that you can command a higher price. Your DV will be either something truly unique (like patented technology) or in your superior execution.*

Differentiation *The process of distinguishing yourself from your competition so you can command higher value and avoid being commoditized or pressured for discounts and concessions.*

Disruption *Your willingness to walk away from an opportunity before it has concluded in order to protect your margins. This willingness disrupts the prospect's buying system, which often relies on a salesperson's commitment to extract concessions and discounts from them.*

Economic democracy *A term describing how an enterprise decides how to prudently invest limited resources and determine which initia-*

tives to fund when there are competing priorities: a dollar's worth of pain equals one vote. The person with the most enterprise-level pain gets the most votes.

Emotional Customer *A person in your prospect organization who feels the pain and consequences of not having your Differentiating Value and needs the pain to end. Targeting the Emotional Customer(s) accelerates the cadence of your sale.*

Inquiry response *One of three possible responses to any question you ask (positive, negative, or inquiry). The inquiry response comes in the form of a question the other person asks for more information and indicates they want to know more.*

Isolation *Isolation is the distance between a decision and its consequences. Isolation allows one party (e.g., the Logical Customer) to make a decision that negatively impacts the enterprise and to remain isolated from the consequences of that decision, because those consequences accrue to another part of the organization (the Emotional Customer). Isolation is always present in a complex sale.*

Last Mile *The final part of a sale (persuading a prospect to change what they're doing) that cannot be accomplished by marketing alone and must be traversed by a human seller. In the Last Mile, the seller runs conversations with the full cast of characters in a prospect organization to alter their decision-making process to value the seller's unique differentiators over competitors' low prices or other concessions.*

Leads *The names of your prospecting targets. You're planning to get their contact info and to get in touch with them, but they're not yet a suspect or a prospect.*

Logical Customer *A person in your prospect organization who has an intellectual relationship to the pain your Differentiating Value can solve. They're often found in Purchasing, Vendor Management, and Information Technology but might be elsewhere in the organization, depending on your DV. Their goal is usually to commoditize vendors and get the lowest price.*

Marketing *The art of getting your company's message about what you're selling into the marketplace. A strategic effort that might include branding, messaging, and advertising. Marketing is "one-to-many" — that is, one single message goes to many people. Marketing can effectively introduce prospects to and raise awareness of your solution and your brand.*

Meeting After the Meeting (MAM) *The meeting held by various stakeholders at your prospect organization to discuss your proposal or offer to do business after you've presented it and have departed. The MAM may be an actual meeting on your prospects' calendars or the process by which these stakeholders ultimately decide what to do with your offer.*

Negative Opening Comment *A simple self-effacing statement that precedes something you say or ask in conversation in order to keep the other person in the OK chair.*

Negative response *One of three possible responses to any question you ask (positive, negative, or inquiry). The negative Response comes* in the form of disagreement or stalls and indicates an unwillingness to further cooperate in the conversation.

Nerdley *Our affectionate name for the Logical Customer who's usually a subject-matter expert.*

Non-Negotiable Weekly Behaviors (NNWB) *The necessary number of Approaches that a seller must make each week in order to ultimately win the number of sales they need to close.*

Open-Ended Question (OEQ) *A question that prompts a rich answer (as opposed to a closed-ended Question that prompts a yes-or-no answer). Any question beginning with words like who, what, when, where, or how is an Open-Ended Question.*

Opportunity cost *Every decision involves an opportunity cost: the next-best option that wasn't chosen in the decision. There are no free moves.*

Pain of change *The pain and risks experienced by a person or enterprise when going through a change, especially any change requiring different behaviors.*

Positive response *One of three possible responses to any question you ask (positive, negative, or inquiry). The positive Response comes in the form of agreement or cooperation and indicates a willingness to move forward with the conversation.*

Presentation *Presenting an offer to do business with a prospect at the very end of the sales process; the offer includes solution details and* *pricing. (Different from a capabilities presentation, which is a high-level overview of the solution's capabilities and might be shown to prospects early in the sales process.)*

Proactive Targeting *Strategically determining who your Emotional and Logical Customers are in your prospect organization, based on the Differentiating Value you bring to the opportunity. This is more efficient than Reactive Targeting.*

Prospects *Your targets who have admitted to having clear motives to change. Having motivation to change is what turns a suspect into a prospect.*

Qualified Selling Opportunity (QSO) *A sales opportunity that you've determined you can win at an acceptable level of commitment of your time and resources. This clarity is accomplished by collecting the Attributes of a QSO in your conversations with the various players in the cast of characters at your prospect organization and waiting to present an offer to do business until all Attributes have been collected.*

Reactive targeting *Determining whether the prospect you've been talking to is a Logical or Emotional Customer based on past conversations and behaviors (as opposed to the more strategic proactive targeting). Can slow down a sale because Logical Customers often masquerade as Emotional Customers, causing sellers who have targeted them Reactively to spend extra time and resources trying to sell to them at Wimp Junction.*

Recognize + Respond *A simple formula to remember that we must always first recognize what the prospect said before responding to it. In* other words, we take care of the other person (by recognizing what they said) before we take care of business (by responding to what they said).

Request for Proposals (RFP) *An RFP is a document issued by an organization seeking to solicit proposals for goods or services from other businesses. The RFP specifies what the organization is looking for and invites businesses to respond with their offers to provide the goods or services sought. They are usually organized by Logical Customers, who will put all potential vendors on a spreadsheet side-by-side, where they all look alike and where lowest price will usually win.*

Reticular Activating System (RAS) *A primal part of the brain related to fight-or-flight responses. Its job is to sort incoming information and discard anything that doesn't either help you achieve your goals (by looking for opportunities to support whatever it thinks is a goal) or keep you alive (by looking for threats to mitigate).*

Selling *The art of persuading a prospect to change what they're doing, with both their cooperation and their consent.*

Selling windows *Your opportunity to sell into a client relationship. When the selling window is open, you can run conversations with your Emotional Customers (and anyone else in the cast of characters you need to be talking to) so that your unique DV continues to be recognized. When the selling window is closed (usually when the client issues an RFP), you're unable to alter the client's evaluation and decision-making processes.*

Situational awareness *A phrase used by military leaders to indicate awareness of one's surroundings, including location, direction, potential* *threats, and potential opportunities. In sales, situational awareness keeps the seller alert to where they are in their selling process, the risks they may encounter in the prospect's buying system, and whom they're talking to (especially whether they're the Emotional or Logical Customer).*

Snipers *In the cast of characters at your prospect organization, snipers are those whose aim is to kill your deal. They usually favor the status quo or the incumbent, and will often show up at your presentation to quietly collect information and ultimately derail your sale, either by taking verbal shots at your solution during the meeting or by saving their fire for the Meeting After the Meeting.*

Suspects *Your prospecting leads with names AND good contact information. Perhaps you've even started talking to them. But they're still just suspects, not Prospects, because they haven't yet indicated any motives to change.*

Think It Over (TIO) *The lie told by prospects to salespeople that they're interested in what's being offered and will "think it over," without committing to next steps. This is the worst possible outcome of any presentation or offer, as it generally means the opportunity has concluded in no sale.*

Total Cost of Ownership Over the Life (TCOOL) *TCOOL is the full cost of purchasing a product or service and includes not only the up-front price but also any additional expenses, fees, repairs, and opportunity costs like lost revenues or missed strategies over the life of the product or service.*

Two-Choice Question *A question that offers a choice between the options presented; a basic example might be, "Is A or B more important to you?"*

Can effectively put two DV points into play with a single question when conversing with an impatient prospect but must be deployed with caution (using Negative Opening Comments and 1-Sentence Stories) to avoid making the other person feel trapped.

Unpaid Consulting   *Providing valuable information and pricing to a prospect, usually in the form of a presentation, demonstration, proposal, or quote, before all the Attributes of a fully Qualified Selling Opportunity have been collected.*

Summary

Ten No-Fail Selling Rules

1. There are no free moves. Ever.
2. Stop telling and start selling.
3. Sell to prospects. Teach customers.
4. Prospects lie with ambiguous, conditional words. Accept none of them.
5. The truth and the money for me only come with clarity.
6. Whenever the prospect asks you to do anything that involves expenditure of your resources, know exactly what will happen next before you do anything.
7. If the prospect can't tell you the cost of the problems, they will not spend money to fix them.
8. Always know where you are in YOUR process.
9. When you're not last to present, you lose.
10. If you didn't create the specifications for the RFP, you are column fodder.

Ten Communication Keys

1. Sell, Don't Tell
2. Nurture, Don't Interrogate
3. Use Open-Ended Questions
4. Don't Ask Why
5. Ask One Question at a Time
6. Get Comfortable with Silence
7. Follow the 80/20 Rule
8. Get Past RAS
9. Know the Culture
10. Soften Your Language

The Five Stages on the right side of the tracks at Wimp Junction

1. Differentiate
2. Target
3. Engage
4. Commit
5. Secure

Nine Call Flow Steps

1. Agreement to the sales process
2. Pain mining and sweeping
3. Confirm order of importance
4. Extract all costs by drilling down
5. Confirm adequate resources
6. Draw out the exact date to begin harvesting the benefits of a solution

7. Confirm that the evaluation and decision-making processes are understood

8. Agree on clear outcomes

9. Attain mutual agreement to move forward

Nine Attributes of a Qualified Selling Opportunity

1. You've gained agreement to the sales process.

2. You've collected pains from the prospect.

3. You've confirmed the order of importance of pains and problems.

4. You've extracted all costs of pains and problems.

5. You've confirmed adequate resources are available.

6. You've drawn out the exact date to begin harvesting the benefits of a solution.

7. You've confirmed their evaluation and decision-making processes.

8. You've agreed on clear outcomes.

9. You've attained mutual agreement to move forward.

Forecast Factors and Weights

- Actionable pain identified: 30%
- Expected spend uncovered and funded: 10%
- Date identified to harvest benefits: 5%
- Evaluation and decision-making processes are understood: 35%
- Commitment gained to move forward: 10%
- Presented and secured: 10%

Acknowledgements

Together, we would like to thank:

Our clients: You are entrepreneurs; you are hardworking leaders; you are hustlers with grit. You inspire and challenge us daily, and this work would never have happened without your insights, questions, and challenges over the last four decades. Thank you.

Our colleagues: The fellow sales trainers, coaches, and consultants who comprehend the high calling and hard challenge of helping people sell well in the marketplace. You have been an endless source of encouragement and inspiration, and you make this work fun. Thank you.

Our book team: Jessica Andersen, editor extraordinaire; Amy Kress, expert graphic designer and brand strategist; Toni Serofin, book designer and publishing maven. We knew almost nothing about bringing a book from idea to reality when we started. We still know almost nothing, but that's okay — we know YOU, and that's all we need. For your guidance, handholding, and brilliance, thank you.

Jennica would like to thank:

Terry: Dad, it's never easy to have a child follow you around asking "Why?" every time you do something, and it can't be any easier when you're both adults working together and she's still picking your brain constantly. Thank you for your patience and for taking the time and effort to explain the deeper concepts to me. It's a privilege to work with you.

Our family: Mom, you promised you would bug me every day until this manuscript was done, and that provided tremendous motivation to get it done in record time; thank you. Keith, you carved out space for me to finish this work even though it meant even less of me at home; I deeply appreciate that and love you. Adelaide, Clarence, and Eloise ... Truth be told, you actually distracted me more often than not from this work, but you're cute, so it was totally worth it; you were also this book's greatest cheering section, and that's the important thing; thank you.

Terry would like to thank:

The IBM Corporation, who interviewed 750 applicants to hire just one salesperson, and then put them through fourteen months of rigorous sales training based on building compelling motivation to pay very premium prices. I'm grateful to have been one of the candidates you took a chance on. We learned to justify our value, walk away from "bottom-feeding price shoppers," and focus on the cast of characters and their process of making a decision. We learned that a 90% closing ratio would keep us employed, and that being last to present would help us get there. We learned to never disparage a competitor, and to build a business case that reframes "cost" and "price." Your investment in a generation of sales trainees is unlike anything in the marketplace today, and I'm forever grateful for your investment in me.

About the Authors

Jennica Dixon grew up watching her father, Terry Slattery, deliver world-class training and consulting at Slattery Sales Group (SSG), where she worked on and off from the time she was twelve years old. After a career in banking and finance, she finally joined SSG full-time in 2020 and is now president of the company. Jennica brings her passion for the Slattery method to her leadership at SSG, empowering great sellers and companies to succeed and close more deals in less time at higher margins. In 2020, Jennica realized she wanted to share the power of Wimp Junction® with a wider audience — so she started writing this book. When she's not coaching her sales clients, Jennica enjoys teaching French to high school students, cooking, and spending time with her husband, their three kids, and their German Shepherd puppy.

Terry Slattery left a successful high-tech sales career to found SSG in 1985, where he still teaches complex sales strategy. Terry has enhanced sales processes and developed value differentiation strategies for clients in more than 100 industries, helping both home-based enterprises and Fortune 100 companies alike to maximize their profit margins. He is also the creator of the groundbreaking Wimp Junction® program that has helped thousands of businesses generate stability and predictable profit in ever-changing economic climates. To date, SSG has helped over 2400 companies and many thousands of salespeople to amplify their efficacy and succeed in complex sales. Away from the office, Terry can be found chasing the winter sun to Arizona and tinkering with jazz piano riffs. He is an avid reader and is known for his many and varied book recommendations.

Download the Wimp Junction companion workbook here:

www.wimpjunction.com/workbook

Made in the USA
Monee, IL
15 April 2024

56990316R00184